One Life to
GIVE

Praise for

ONE LIFE TO GIVE

"Reading *One Life to Give* is truly a gift to oneself—a profound and rivet-
ing experience that kept me up into the late hours following a journey both
immensely provocative and transformative. Andrew Bienkowski gives fully
of himself in this book, with a power that brings forth a spirit of healing
so important at this time in our world. I'm already recommending this to
everyone I know."

—STEPHAN RECHTSCHAFFEN, MD, co-founder,
Omega Institute and Blue Spirit Costa Rica

"I was touched by this story of courage and sacrifice, blended with gems
of wisdom reflecting the author's many years as a psychotherapist. I found
myself highlighting many excellent points throughout its pages."

—DAN MILLMAN, author of *Way of the Peaceful Warrior*

"*One Life to Give* is a compelling and heartwarming saga that will inspire,
uplift, and move you to appreciate your loved ones and consider what you
can contribute rather than get. Andrew Bienkowski brings a lifetime of
experience as a soulful therapist to his account, and for that I am deeply
grateful. Anyone who values family, or feels disconnected from loved ones,
would benefit immensely from this extraordinary book and the powerful,
practical lessons it bestows."

—ALAN COHEN, author of *Linden's Last Life*

THE EXPERIMENT

BECAUSE EVERY BOOK IS A TEST OF NEW IDEAS

One Life to
GIVE

A PATH TO FINDING YOURSELF
BY HELPING OTHERS

ANDREW BIENKOWSKI
with MARY AKERS

FOREWORD BY GORDON LIVINGSTON, MD

THE EXPERIMENT

NEW YORK

THE EXPERIMENT, LLC
260 FIFTH AVENUE
NEW YORK, NY 10001–6425
WWW.THEEXPERIMENTPUBLISHING.COM

ORIGINALLY PUBLISHED IN somewhat different form in Australia in 2008 as
Radical Gratitude by Inspired Living, an imprint of Allen & Unwin.
The eight photographs on pages 206–207 are courtesy of Andrew Bienkowski.

LIBRARY OF CONGRESS Control Number: 2009937035
ISBN 978-1-61519-008-9

COVER DESIGN BY Chin-Yee Lai
COVER PHOTOGRAPH © PPSOP/Corbis
DESIGN BY Pauline Neuwirth, Neuwirth & Associates, Inc.

MANUFACTURED IN THE United States of America
FIRST PRINTING JANUARY 2010

10 9 8 7 6 5 4 3 2 1

For DZIADEK, *my grandfather, who gave his life for me, and in doing so, taught me how to live.*

CONTENTS

WISDOM IS A hard-won virtue. What we make of the adversities with which life inevitably confronts us determines whether we have anything useful to say to those who follow us. Andrew Bienkowski passes the test with this extraordinary story of his childhood exile to Siberia and the lessons he learned there about loyalty, perseverance, gratitude, and love. That he was later able to convey these insights to others in a long career as a psychotherapist is a natural outcome of his conclusion that our obligation in life is to take what we have learned and "pay it forward." This book reflects his determination to give permanent form to truths about living that come only with experience and reflection.

If he is correct that "powerlessness is the disease of our times," then we must all consider our sources of strength and determination. What will sustain us as we search for the meaning of our lives? Absent a religious formula to guide us, what do we have that justifies our time on the planet and enables us to nourish optimism in the face of our mortality? The answer, Bienkowski suggests, lies in what we are able to give others: understanding, tolerance, faith, and that form of love that we call kindness.

The clinical vignettes that the author uses to describe how he has helped people struggle with their problems in living illuminate the power of empathic listening and the ability to be fully present with another person as they find sometimes surprising solutions that are wholly their own. What is required in these healing interactions is usually not some blinding insight, sage advice, or magical medication. Rather, we as therapists bear compassionate witness to exercises in courage and the rebirth of hope. It is useful in this process if the person seeking help senses that the putative helper has himself confronted adversity in his own life and drawn from it the lesson that it is not what happens to us that determines our futures, but how we respond.

As you read this book think about the Siberia that comes to each of us sooner or later. Our own trials most often take the form of rejection, loss, depression, illness, or, if we are lucky, the depredations of age. None of us is immune to adversity, and none of us gets out of here alive. It is what we do with these experiences that defines us as people and decides the outcome of our two great and intertwined searches—

for happiness and love. The profound message that this book contains is not new but deserves repeating: the last human freedom is the choice of how we confront our fates. May you meet your own with the grace and generosity with which this author and his family faced theirs.

⁓

GORDON LIVINGSTON, MD, a psychiatrist and writer, is the author of four books—*Only Spring: On Mourning the Death of My Son*, *And Never Stop Dancing: Thirty More True Things You Need to Know Now*, *How to Love*, and the internationally bestselling *Too Soon Old, Too Late Smart: Thirty True Things You Need to Know Now*. He lives and works in Columbia, Maryland.

AUTHORS' NOTES

I'VE ALWAYS HAD a great thirst for learning. And I've always known that the most important lessons of my life were learned in Siberia—that my purpose and core philosophy were formed during that difficult time. Originally, my attempts to write this book focused on teaching the reader how to be more effective in helping others—passing on my lifetime of skills to anyone who had an interest in helping his fellow man. That original version was more like a textbook or a manual. I quickly realized that a book like that would not interest many readers.

Although I did not want this book to be *about* me, Mary Akers helped me to see that my life story and professional experience would serve to dramatize the life lessons I longed to pass on to readers. However, I am not a writer and my stories from Siberia were like photographs as seen in black and white. What Mary did with her wonderful writing skills was to put color into those pictures. She brought the stories to life. It's been a delightful experience working with her, creating this book. When I look at our creation now, I realize that most of the credit should go to her.

—*Andrew Bienkowski*

THE SIBERIAN STORIES included in this book represent the sort of family lore that gets passed down from generation to generation. Many of the accounts originated with Andrew Bienkowski's grandmother, Babcia, who understood the healing power of a good story well told and refused to let hers languish in the dark cave of memory. Babcia's fierce determination to retell her experiences ensured that her grandchildren would remember their mother after her untimely death, that the sacrifices of their grandfather would continue to shape their lives, and that they would understand the evils that can beset ordinary, innocent citizens when governments exert too much power over ideology and individual will.

The stories from Siberia that did not originate with Babcia are based on the fractured memories of Andy's own childhood experiences, as recalled by him and conveyed to me. Together we spent many hours poring over old family photographs, discussing the past, and reliving the events that helped his family survive their traumatic ordeal. As in any enterprise based solely on memory, there are bound to be discrepancies. But we believe we have portrayed the trials that his family faced with as much accuracy and fidelity as possible. Specific sensory details have been reimagined to enhance the reader's experience, but the basic events depicted are unchanged.

While writing, I propped a photograph of Andy's grandfather beside my computer. It was taken about a month before his death and is from an official Russian identification document. In it, his eyes stare out past the camera, past the Russian official photographing him, toward me, seventy years into the future. He is admonishing me to *get it right*, to *tell it true*. And so I spent many hours imagining the unimaginable: what Andy felt at five years old, foraging for mushrooms that barely kept his family from starvation; what his grandfather felt as he purposefully wasted away on his deathbed; how his grandmother reacted to a Russian soldier's death threats. Collectively, the Siberia stories in *One Life to Give* represent my efforts to understand, respect, and accurately portray the members of Andy's family and the trials they endured. It was a daunting task. I hope I succeeded.

—Mary Akers

One Life to
GIVE

1.

Radical Gratitude

Poverty taught me that all was not well under the sun;
but the sun taught me that poverty was not everything.

—ALBERT CAMUS

IT WAS THE winter of 1940 and Vladislav Paluchowski had
been hungry for weeks. A great, burning hunger ate up his
insides. Lack of sustenance made him see strange things,
like visions of flesh evaporating from his bones, rising into
thin air, traveling up through shafts of sunlight. He knew
the hunger brought the visions, but oddly enough, the images comforted him.

Outside, the real sun had long since surrendered its
few hours of daylight, setting to a light gray cast: Siberia
in winter. The wind raced across the frozen plain and
moaned through the hut the family had been fortunate
enough to find and inhabit, back when the old man was

still strong, still the head of the family, before the hunger consumed him.

This morning, using several precious pats of dried cow dung, his wife made a fire and moved his straw bed closer, but it didn't matter. The only warmth the old man felt anymore came from the great, white-hot fire in his belly and the burning fire of his spirit.

When food and water were presented to him for the thirteenth time in as many days, the old man used the last of his energy to turn his head away. In his mind he grabbed his belt and cinched it tighter against a stomach that had long since ceased to rumble, only creaking occasionally now, like an old door, rusty on its hinges. As the man's strength ebbed, he felt his body sink deeper into the straw and envisioned the future his grandchildren would have, the future that his death would help ensure.

In tough times Vladislav had always turned inward, toward a greater strength—strength of faith, of wisdom, and of sacrifice. He had long before calculated how much food the five of them would need in order to survive the winter and he knew there wouldn't be enough to sustain them all. The time had come. To save the others—his wife, his daughter, his two grandsons—he would give up his already meager portions.

The women—eyes long since drained of tears and exhausted from worry and work and lack of food themselves—no longer had the energy to object. The two young boys knew to respect the wishes of adults and so said nothing. But they watched. This old man wasn't just a husband and father. He wasn't just a grandfather. He was a force of nature. To starve was his dying wish, and he would not be denied.

To Vladislav, it was a simple question of fact: Who would be most useful to the children? He had protected them as best he could, through banishment from their Polish homeland, through the long, dirty train ride that he thought would surely kill them, through moving their scant belongings into this small mud hut, and now his last remaining duty was to save the children. All of those other jobs had been taxing. All had been difficult. By contrast, his current job was simple.

His job was to die.

WHEN TIMES GET difficult, I often think of that old man out there on the steppe, making his final, fatal decision. The decision that would touch and change every one of the people for whom he made the ultimate sacrifice. I think of how the decision must have been difficult for him, and yet, also, in a strange way, so very clear. That man's life, and especially his death, have been a great inspiration to me. Of the five people who lived in that mud hut, and the four who survived to leave the steppe, I am the only remaining member still alive.

That man was my grandfather, and the child he died to save was me.

Perhaps because of my grandfather's early sacrifice, witnessed at the impressionable age of five, I have always had trouble with the "me first" approach of our modern world. Helping the self is only the first part of the equation. It is not what ultimately sustains an individual. As Winston Churchill famously said, "We make a living by what we get, we make a life by what we give."

Thankfully, most of us will never be called upon to make as great a sacrifice as my grandfather made, but we *can* make smaller, daily sacrifices. We can learn to put others first in ways that create joy and enhance our lives. By sharing my Siberian experiences with you (and drawing on four decades as a practicing psychotherapist), I hope—in writing this book—to inspire you to nurture one of your greatest human attributes: the ability to understand and help others.

Ironically, one of the best ways to cultivate a desire to help others is to practice being *purposefully grateful* ourselves. Spending even a little time each day focusing on the things we have to be grateful for improves all aspects of our lives. And it's so simple!

Actively cultivating gratefulness is not something most of us spend much time on. We are more prone to focus on our *wants* than on our *haves*. But this is not the only way to approach the world. We could easily wake up every morning thinking, "I have breath! I have life! I have shelter! I am here!" These are grand things to celebrate and should not be taken for granted.

And yet we do.

The alarm sounds and we roll over and climb out of bed and begin to trudge through another day. But think, for a moment, about a day in which we wake and remember what we *already* have, the blessings that we have already been given, the things that we have already earned, the love that we have already found. Imagine a morning when we wake up and celebrate the *now*.

Remember this: *If you are in a position to take things for granted, you are already blessed beyond your needs.*

In today's world, where commerce is king, we are bombarded by advertising designed with the sole intent of creating a sense of dissatisfaction and longing—in short, to make us want the elusive *more*. This general sense of dissatisfaction keeps us from seeing the abundant good that already surrounds us. It keeps us trapped in the illusion that we could be satisfied if we only had just a little bit more. But the trouble with satisfaction is that it is a constantly receding horizon. There is always the *more,* the *bigger,* and the *better* located just beyond our reach.

To practice gratitude, we must tune out these negative messages and look for the miracle in every day. We must tell ourselves stories that remind us that each day—each moment—is a precious gift. And that gift is what we have now, today, not something we need to look for in a far distant future.

There is a Sanskrit proverb that says, "Yesterday is but a dream, tomorrow is only a vision. But today, well lived, makes every yesterday a dream of happiness, and every tomorrow a vision of hope. Look well, therefore, to this day, for it is life, the very life of life."

If we can live in gratefulness today, the regrets of the past and the worries of the future disappear. By *practicing* gratefulness, we move out of the self, we slow down and appreciate the present. And the more we practice gratefulness, the more grateful we become. Like wearing a pair of glasses whose lenses continually sharpen, we find more and more things to be grateful for. When you wear your gratitude glasses every day, they become a part of who you are— a habit of being.

I am grateful not only to my grandfather, for his sacrifice, but even for the awful experiences of our time in Siberia. Why? Because of the gifts that those horrifying experiences have given me, the understanding that they imparted. I am a better person for having suffered.

As a concept, I call this "radical gratitude." It is the idea that we can learn to feel grateful, even for the terrible things that happen to us in our lives. More simply put, it is a version of the old adage, "That which does not kill us makes us stronger." Assuming you want to be stronger, you can find a sense of gratitude, even in suffering.

Although we would like to know a world without pain, without suffering, we will not. The very act of being born is a painful separation—our very first. Life then proceeds as a series of lessons, some of which will inevitably be painful: *the stove is hot, the blade is sharp, people disappoint us.* But beyond the pain lies understanding: *don't touch the stove, wield the knife with care, learn whom to trust.*

This pain is how we learn and grow as humans. Kahlil Gibran wrote, "Your pain is the breaking of the shell that encloses your understanding. Even as the stone of the fruit must break, that its heart may stand in the sun, so must you know pain." Once we accept the message that pain is a necessary part of life, we open the door to radical gratitude.

I suggest radical gratitude as a first step on the path to finding yourself by helping others not because I learned it first—I didn't, it took years to get there—but because the feeling of grace that radical gratitude provides is what made all the other steps possible.

Of course, we do not look forward to the difficult times in our lives. We do not welcome suffering. But radical gratitude is not experienced in the midst of suffering; it is only recognizable in hindsight. Once we look back at the difficult times, appreciate how far we have come, and admire where we are today, only then are we open to the healing that radical gratitude offers.

Helen Keller, blind and deaf from infancy, surely understood suffering. She also overcame it, learning to sign, read, and write. And I am thankful that she did, for she has left behind a great legacy of wisdom. "Character cannot be developed in ease and quiet," she wrote. "Only through experience of trial and suffering can the soul be strengthened, ambition inspired, and success achieved."

Once we understand the value of suffering, and that its annealing fire has the power to strengthen us, we learn to accept the difficulties life throws our way, and we learn to see past the trying times to a promise of greater strength and understanding. The hope lies in the lessons that our struggles impart. And they can transform us.

⁓

IN HIS FINAL days, Vladislav's hunger became greater than any hunger he had ever known. The occasional missed meal paled in comparison. This hunger soared past that of being sent to bed without supper as a child. It was all-consuming. But he never felt hopeless. Despite his dire circumstances, he was full of hope. It was hope that had made him refuse all food—hope for the future, hope for his grandchildren.

As the tiny fire in the grate burned down, the spark in the old man's eyes glowed brighter. A sense of calm filled the room, but the old man was not yet fully at peace. He had one thing more he needed to say. In that dim, cold room, his white hair shone and his eyes burned. He lifted his head from the straw and whispered, "*Pochowajcie mnie nagim*"

The family gathered closer, the better to hear over the noise of the wind. They held his hands; his skin was cool and papery thin. They touched his face. It had been days since he had spoken and they knew these words might be his last. They also knew that when the old man spoke, he spoke of important things. He did not waste words.

"What is it, grandfather?" The older child, only six years old, stepped forward to assume his new place in the family, sensing his beloved Dziadek's approaching death.

Again the old man said, "*Pochowajcie mnie nagim*" This time he spoke loudly enough so that all could hear: "Bury me naked." The family looked to one another in confusion. Had they heard correctly? This thing he was asking of them felt like the ultimate act of disrespect. He had been an important man in Poland. He had been respected and admired. They could not understand why he would request such a demeaning end to his life.

As his wife began to shake her head in refusal, the old man continued. "These clothes," he said. "Sell them." His voice was barely a whisper. "Sell them. And eat."

⁓

I MAY HAVE been only a small child when we granted my grandfather's unusual dying wish, but I will never forget the sacrifices he made. I am grateful to have had this chance at life, this chance that he helped to give me. From the bottom of my heart, I thank you, Dziadek.

I talk about suffering in this book not to focus on the negative but to increase *awareness*. It is very important that we not forget that suffering exists. We need not dwell on it, but as Albert Schweitzer counseled, "Think occasionally of the suffering of which you spare yourself the sight." Remembering that we all suffer helps to keep us human. It helps to keep us grateful.

There is one simple source of gratefulness that we can all tap into: the contributions of those who have come before us. No matter where we are in our lives, we owe a debt of gratitude to pioneering people who paved the way, ancestors who gave us life, reformists who insisted on a better form of government, inventors who have improved the quality of life, scientists who worked to cure disease—in short, people whose contributions have made our lives easier, better, or even possible. These people do not ask us to be grateful, but we should be. And the best way to express our gratitude to those who have gone before us is to pay it forward. We can express our gratitude by working to make the world a better place in the same way that others have made it a better place for us. As the saying goes, we must plant trees under whose shade we do not intend to sit.

There is a wonderful book by Gregg Krech, titled *Nai-kan*, which teaches a Japanese way of practicing gratitude. Krech instructs individuals and groups to learn to develop a natural sense of gratitude "for all the blessings bestowed on us by others, blessings that were always there but went unnoticed." He suggests we take a moment to consider the (approximately) ten thousand times our mothers or some other caregiver changed our diapers when we were babies. We did nothing to deserve this—it was simply done for us because we needed it to be done. We were fed three meals each day by someone who cared enough to see that we did not go hungry. Someone first worked to earn money, then took that money to the store, shopped for food, carried it home, cooked it for us, served us, and cleaned up after us, only to begin the entire process again. In short, we were provided for. We were cared for. Most likely, we were also loved.

It is important in this exercise not to qualify the care: whether you were cared for perfectly is not the issue. That you were cared for at all, is. When we take the time to realize how much others have done for us, how interconnected we all are, how dependent we are on others for our very survival, then our own attitude originates with gratitude, with a desire to give back.

Another key aspect of experiencing gratitude is learning to see that what we have *right now* is enough. It is easy to be grateful for the gifts that astound, that take our breath away. It is more difficult when the gifts are average, or even routine—as the gift of a parent going off to work each day to earn money, or preparing a meal for all to eat.

It is important that we remember to take note of the things in our lives that are quite simply *good enough*. This is where grace lies. There is a quote from the Buddha's teachings that perfectly expresses this notion: "Let us rise up and be thankful, for if we didn't learn a lot today, at least we learned a little, and if we didn't learn a little, at least we didn't get sick, and if we got sick, at least we didn't die; so, let us all be thankful."

Many people believe that they are what they have become over the years and that they cannot change their attitudes. Having seen hundreds of people change in significant ways over the course of my professional lifetime, I disagree. I have seen people who were angry or fearful become, with time and effort, calm and content. I have witnessed people who were dissatisfied and restless learn to live their lives with conscious gratitude and cultivate happiness. The key element in each of these cases was *intention*.

I learned the importance of intention from a Native American elder. He taught me that in order to change, one's intention has to be very specific and clearly stated every day. Intending to "do better" or "be a good person" is not specific enough, and can be daunting even to consider. But stating, "My intention is to be patient today," or "My intention is to be nonjudgmental" is easier because it is concrete and specific. By stating the goal simply, we make it attainable.

When we reaffirm our specific intention every day, it becomes integrated into our being and then is manifested in our behavior. Simply telling yourself, "Today, I intend to be grateful," will help you be open to small acts of kindness and actively seek occasions to express your gratitude to others. To become more grateful, we must learn to take nothing for granted. It is often the people who have experienced the greatest suffering in the world who are also the most grateful. This is because they have learned that what they have is not a given—they take nothing for granted. They are grateful for what they have today and every day.

"To educate yourself for the feeling of gratitude means to take nothing for granted," said Albert Schweitzer. "Nothing that is done for you is a matter of course. Everything originates in a will for the good, which is directed at you. Train yourself never to put off the word or action for the expression of gratitude." Once we learn to actively seek reasons to be grateful, we suddenly find them everywhere. And when we learn to focus *intention* on our own gratitude, gratitude becomes a way of life and our efforts to help others become natural and spontaneous.

Once you have learned to access the healing power of radical gratitude, you will find that the fullness of life greets you at every turn. What we have, we suddenly realize, is enough—more than enough. The sticky problem turns unexpectedly into a solution, the loss reveals itself to be a gain, the failure simply success in another realm. Once we learn to accept the transformation that radical gratitude bestows, all of life's possibilities open up to us.

Radical gratitude allows us to make sense of and accept the past, to embrace and find peace in the present, and it creates a vision of hope for the future. Studies have shown that grateful people are happier people—more helpful, more forgiving, and less depressed. By simply taking an attitude of gratitude toward the world, ourselves, and others, we can actually cultivate our own happiness and sense of well-being.

When we remember the many things in our lives for which we *can* be grateful (yes, even the painful experiences) and spend a bit of time and energy each day on practicing gratitude, gratefulness becomes a way of life. And the ability to focus on the good, to feel grateful, to practice gratefulness, is within each one of us. When we consciously choose to acknowledge and share our gratitude, we see how quickly gratitude grows and spreads to others. We begin to understand—once gratitude opens the door—that we are all connected.

2.

We Are All Connected

You will find that the mere resolve not to be useless,
and the honest desire to help other people, will, in the
quickest and delicatest ways, improve yourself.
—JOHN RUSKIN

VLADISLAV KNEW HE had very little time left. As the pain
began to leave his body, in its place settled a bright, white
clarity. His thoughts returned to 1939 and the section of
Poland where he lived with his wife and family—where his
daughter and her husband had a home, where his grandchildren played and laughed and attended school.

That fall the city of Lvov, where he lived, was taken over
by the Russian government. Stalin instructed his military
forces to deport more than one million Polish citizens to
Siberia. The deported Poles were deemed undesirable citizens of the new Soviet communist territory and so were cast
out. Many, like Vladislav and his family, were banished sim-

ply because they were seen as a threat, because their education and wealth made them resistant to communism. They were awakened in the middle of the night and given ten minutes to pack.

Five members of Vladislav's family were expelled: his wife Babcia, his daughter Zosia, his two young grandsons, and himself. His son-in-law, an officer in the Polish army, had been fighting against the Germans in the west when Russia invaded Poland from the east and was now being held as a prisoner-of-war.

Vladislav and his wife Babcia had anticipated their banishment, and for weeks the family had been hoarding dried food and small valuables. Each adult was allowed a single suitcase. The family members were transported by military vehicle and loaded at gunpoint onto a crowded cattle car in a long train of cattle cars.

In that dim, dirty cattle car, they traveled for three weeks with no heat, no food, and no clear understanding of what they were heading toward. The only bathroom was a small hole in the floor at the center of the car. Many times during the journey, the train squealed to a stop and the massive cargo door slid open with a metallic groan. Light streamed in on the blinking passengers. During these stops, a bucket of water was passed among the passengers, each of whom was allowed a small sip only. Any heat that had accumulated from the close quarters vanished as frigid air blew into the car. Any passengers who had died were lifted by the arms and legs and heaved out onto the frozen ground.

Then the heavy doors groaned shut and the train rumbled on.

⌒

DURING THAT AWFUL, long train ride we had no idea where we were going or what awaited us. Everyone in the car was frightened, many were despondent, and still others were hysterical. And even as a child I had a sense of wanting so badly to help them.

Some of those who were banished hadn't even made it aboard the train—they panicked during the boarding and attempted to run away. Those who fled were shot in the back as they ran. We could do nothing to help.

I remember the faces of the soldiers, too, how they showed no emotion when they shot the running people. It was a startling sight and inspired a great deal of fear in those of us still waiting to board the train. I believe this first awful experience was the beginning of my intense lifelong desire to help others in need.

Amazing acts of kindness took place on that train, as well as desperate acts of self-preservation. As I observed the struggles all around me, I began to understand that we must help one another if we are all to survive, and that we all have a role in that survival. We are all connected.

If we embrace such thinking, a natural desire to give back and help others develops within us. Albert Schweitzer, a witness to great suffering himself, said, "You must give some time to your fellow men. Even if it's a little thing, do something for others—something for which you get no pay but the privilege of doing it."

For more than forty years I have made it my life's work to help others, but in reality, most of the people I have helped already had the solution within themselves, or at least had a sense of what course of action they should follow. What they didn't know was how to access the answer that was already within them. In working with them, my role became that of *facilitator* rather than solver.

In fact, if a client asks me for advice, I tell them I can't give them any. If they persist, I tell them that there are only four outcomes when advice is given, and all of them are negative. If I give advice, it is taken, and the outcome is *good,* the client is not empowered because he sees me as the fixer of his problems. If I give advice, it is taken, and the outcome is *bad*, the client becomes angry with me for giving bad advice and with himself for taking it. If I give advice, it is *not* taken, and the outcome is *good,* the client is empowered to listen to himself, but resents me for giving what he now believes must have been bad advice. And if I give advice, it is *not* taken, and the outcome is *bad*, then the client feels he should have taken my advice after all, and he is not empowered.

Rather than dispense advice, it is far better to encourage a partnership between equals wherein each partner contributes to achieving the solution. In this way, feelings of dependency and inadequacy are minimized. Creating a problem-solving partnership can be encouraged in the following ways.

Pay attention to language. The language people use is how they feel most comfortable being addressed. If a person speaks informally, pattern your responses in informal speech; if he tends towards more formal speech, adjust your speech accordingly. Your responses will be better received if they match his presentation.

Pay attention to tone. Just as you want to be sensitive to language, your responses should match the tone of the person you seek to help. If your friend is despondent and speaks in a depressed tone, you don't want to give fast, cheerful responses. Matching your tone more closely to hers will show that you respect her position and empathize with her feelings.

Respond. It is important to let your friend do most of the talking, but don't stay silent for too long. Even in the midst of a lengthy explanation, you can ask the occasional question to clarify your understanding and ensure that the conversation does not become entirely one-sided.

Offer a symbolic comparison. You may find it helpful to restate what your friend has said, using a symbol as a reference. A phrase such as, "You feel as if you've wandered off the path," or "You feel like a boat that's been set adrift," may get to his feelings in a way that validates his emotions but allows him to remain comfortable with the discussion.

Self-disclose. One very effective way to encourage rapport is to practice self-disclosure. This means that you tell the person you are trying to help about any times you have been in a similar situation or had similar feelings. Your reference should be brief so as to keep the focus on your friend's problem, but self-disclosure gives your point of view extra credence, as "someone who's been there."

Often when we reach out to others in this way, with gratitude as our starting point, we begin to fully understand the meaning of the phrase, "There but for the grace of God go I." We begin to realize that we are not so different from our suffering brothers and sisters, we are not separate from our surroundings, and in fact, we are all connected. When we recognize this oneness that we share, we learn to see the world not as something separate from us but as a part of us. As a part of the oneness that surrounds us. And so what we do for others, we ultimately do for ourselves, for our world. Christ instructed his followers in this way: "As you have done it unto the least among us, you have done it unto me." This is a wonderful and powerful expression of our connectedness.

Once we begin to understand that we are all intricately linked in this great web of life, a desire to reach out to others grows within us and we understand the importance of giving back. Albert Einstein expressed it this way: "Only a life lived for others is a life worth living."

Once you give back to the world on a regular basis, you will notice how contagious it becomes, how easily it grows and spreads. The person that you help is often made to feel so good that he will turn around and help two more people, who in turn help two more, and so on. In this way we can "pay it forward" and create a movement that helps the world exponentially.

Like a mother who is "born" the moment her baby enters the world, the helper is "born" at the moment he helps another. If you are reading this, you are probably someone who already has years of experience in dealing with difficult situations. You have learned from those experiences and you use your skills as new situations arise. It is my sincere hope that reading this book will give you the confidence and encouragement to take it one step further.

VLADISLAV'S FAMILY STAYED close together in the cattle car. As the train clattered along, he peered through the cracks between the boards. He caught fleeting glimpses of a bleak countryside. He wondered what would become of his family. He carefully portioned out the food.

During those long, awful weeks, Vladislav and his wife Babcia worked to keep the family as comfortable and optimistic as possible in the cramped cattle car, surrounded by other anxious exiles, rattling across the Siberian wasteland headed toward an unknown fate. They sat and slept close together, huddling for warmth and comfort.

Their fellow passengers reacted to the banishment in many different ways. Some became angry and indignant, loudly demanding to know where they were being taken, when they would have food, when they would be allowed off. There was no one to answer the questions, but still they asked.

Some tried to make friends with their fellow passengers, attempted to lighten the mood, or share opinions and experiences, making connections with others to help them understand where they were being sent and why.

Some huddled in tight, quiet groups, whispering anxiously, not speaking to the passengers around them but holding tightly to their own belongings and to their family members.

Some entered the car alone and crept off by themselves, curling their bodies into tight balls, ignoring not only the other passengers on the train but also any conversation, any offers of assistance, and any gestures of friendship. Most often, these were the first to die.

At each small village, the train stopped and a group of exiles was forced off, left to fend for themselves or die of starvation, disease, and cold. That interminable train ride finally ended for Vladislav and his family when they were dumped unceremoniously into the Siberian countryside with a small collection of mud huts visible in the distance. Even before the train resumed its clattering journey, the family retrieved their meager belongings and began to walk.

They suffered a great deal that winter. As outsiders in that small communist village, they were looked down upon by their neighbors as they competed for the same limited resources. The mud hut they occupied was small, ten feet by ten feet. The floor was dirt, the hut extremely cold. There was no furniture. And worse, especially for the children, there were whole days with no food at all. The family was slowly starving.

Out on the vast snow-covered plain, the wolves were starving, too. They howled restlessly in the distance, they moved across the steppe in a search for food that brought them to the edge of the village, to the threshold of Vladislav's mud hut. They prowled the perimeter. They grew bolder, moving closer until they were just outside; their howls echoed through the hut as the family huddled inside. The hungriest wolves scratched at the door. No one in the village went outside on winter nights.

Facing the realities of extremely little food, an uncertain future, the ever-present threat of dwindling fuel, loss of contact with the outside world, and a very literal wolf-at-the-door experience, Vladislav realized that no help would be forthcoming, and if they were to survive, the family members would have to help each other. With a heavy heart, he also understood the way in which he could best help his loved ones survive the horrors of Siberia.

MY GRANDFATHER MADE the decision to put our needs before his own and paid for it with his life. To honor his sacrifice, I have in turn aspired to make my life meaningful to the world. One of the best ways I have found to do this is by sharing my time and talents. Even as a small child I understood that helping other people was a worthy goal. I learned that when we help others, everyone benefits. My whole family understood this, and each one of us assumed a role in feeding the family and staying alive. From picking up dried cow dung for fuel, to picking berries in the spring or mushrooms in the fall, there was something for everyone to do to participate in our survival. We had to help each other in order to stay alive.

As a way to help visualize our human connectedness, I tell my patients the following story: Picture yourself entering a room filled with hungry people. In this room, there are tables loaded with all types of wonderful foods—foods that must be eaten with a spoon. The only problem is that the spoons provided are three feet long. Because of this, no one can eat; the mood in the room is one of dissatisfaction, anger, and frustration.

Now leave that room and enter the room beside it. In this room, the same situation is in place—delicious food everywhere and only three-foot spoons to eat it with. But in this room, the people are happy. They are laughing and eating. How? How did they manage to eat with three-foot spoons? Simple. They are feeding each other.

Which room would you rather visit?

Helping others is an activity that most of us enjoy—humans are compassionate creatures, after all—but sometimes fear or uncertainty can keep us from helping. Perhaps we long to offer condolences, but don't, for fear of doing it clumsily, or of making the pain worse. We may doubt our own ability to help effectively, or perhaps we fear the embarrassment of having our help rejected. In some cases, we may even be afraid of unpleasant repercussions. What we must remember, though, is that even a clumsy gesture is better than none at all. And the best way to become less clumsy? Practice, of course. The more you push aside your fear and make an attempt, the better and more skilled your future attempts become.

After I became a therapist and began the business of professional helping, I was reintroduced to a painful lesson—a lesson I first experienced on that long, difficult train ride into Siberia: No matter how much we may wish to help others, not every individual *can* be helped. I believe there are at least five specific categories of people who cannot be helped.

We all know someone for whom suffering seems to be a way of life. Relationships go sour, jobs are repeatedly lost, and money is always tight. In short, misfortune seems to follow like a black cloud. Such an individual will spend a great deal of time speaking of his unhappiness and will recount his misfortunes in detail. It is a natural, human impulse to want to help such a person, but if we try and fail, it is important to understand that this person is *attached to suffering* on a very deep level. He will not surrender it, no matter the efforts you make on his behalf.

I once had a patient I'll call Joe. Joe came to me because his life was in utter chaos. He drank to excess every night and often ended up in fistfights. As a result, Joe spent many days battered and bruised. He would get fired from jobs after only a few weeks, evicted from apartments, and dumped by girlfriends. It was clear that Joe needed some stability. We worked very hard together for many months and his life stabilized dramatically. By all accounts, Joe had concluded a successful round of therapy. All accounts except Joe's, that is. Within a few months, Joe fell back into his old habits. He told me he couldn't stand his new life; it had become too boring. A person this wedded to his problems should not and possibly *cannot* be interfered with.

Another patient, "Patricia," had been physically abused by her previous eight boyfriends. By her own account, she was miserable: physically battered, emotionally distraught. I had a great deal of sympathy for her and worked hard to get her to change her thinking. Yet as soon as Patricia encountered a man who was interested in her and was also gentle, nonviolent, and dependable, she lost interest. She would describe him as "boring." Sadly, Patricia was so wedded to her suffering that she could not become interested in a relationship unless it brought some promise of physical or emotional pain.

When people are heavily committed to suffering, there is a very strong defense against eliminating that suffering.

A person may be suffering a tremendous amount, and the therapist may be doing everything in his power to help that person, but the more the therapy continues the more clearly comes the message that this individual has a tremendous attachment, on a very deep level, to suffering. Accepting that you have encountered such a person and letting go your desire to help does not mean you have failed. Even a trained professional therapist can be of only minimal help to such an individual.

Another situation best left to a professional is the suicidal individual. A person who expresses suicidal thoughts needs professional help and should be encouraged to see a mental health provider immediately. If you do find yourself dealing with a suicidal individual, you can attempt to deescalate the importance of whatever is triggering the episode. People in a deeply depressed state need help recognizing that such things come in cycles, and while there may not appear to be a way out at that moment, sooner or later relief from the situation will arrive.

Third, an individual who is under the influence of drugs or alcohol cannot be helped unless he first gives up the alcohol or drugs. It is only after he, by his own choice, gives up the addictive behavior that he can be helped. It is better not to try working with an addict unless you are a professional who is properly trained to handle such problems.

In his book *People of the Lie,* Scott Peck discusses a fourth category of patients who cannot be helped. These people hide behind a façade of respectability, created by lies. They lie to others and to themselves. Their actions are destructive and they do not accept any responsibility for their behavior. These individuals are uncomfortable to be around. Chances are, if you feel uncomfortable with someone, you won't be very effective in helping them. It is better to expend your energies elsewhere and let these individuals struggle with their own virulent demons.

Finally, there is the person who can't be helped because he or she refuses help. This, too, must be recognized. Even when someone is giving a very clear message, "I don't need your help, I don't want your help," we may keep stubbornly trying because we see that person as someone who truly does need assistance. But it is important to recognize the don't-help-me message, and it is essential that we accept and honor it. Otherwise, we become "do-gooders" and are more interfering than helpful.

If encountering someone who can't be helped leaves *you* feeling helpless, remember that there are still many others who *can* be helped. And for those who can't, there are still other ways to reach out. We are all connected in this great web of life and consciousness, and when we can do nothing else for someone, we can still send unconditional love and good thoughts their way. We may lack the specific skills to help troubled individuals on a physical level, but we can help from a distance through prayer, meditation, and visualizations.

When we remember that we are all connected—in our survival and in our consciousness—we can *choose* to be a beacon of love and kindness, we can visualize our troubled loved ones surrounded by light, love, and happiness, and we *can* make a difference. And our first step on that path to learning how thoroughly we are connected must be to listen intently.

3.

Listen Intently and You Will Learn

It is the province of knowledge to speak, and it is the
privilege of wisdom to listen.

—OLIVER WENDELL HOLMES

VLADISLAV'S FAMILY HAD heard his dying wish and—
against their own desires—granted it. He would be buried
naked. His clothes would be sold for food and the family
would eat. Carefully and lovingly they wrapped his emaci-
ated body in a blanket and placed it on a borrowed cart that
they drove far into the plain for his burial.

The day was cold and the ground was frozen hard. The
family, weakened from hunger and from the long and difficult
deathbed watch, struggled to penetrate the frozen ground.
They dug as far into the permafrost as they were able and gathered many rocks. Silently, they struggled to lift the old man's
body out of the cart and lower it into the shallow grave.

They did their best to provide a brief ceremony, but the women were weakened, the children were cold and hungry, and the horse and cart needed to be returned to their owner. The family had already spent too long in the digging. They uttered final words of love and piled the gathered stones atop the thin covering of earth over Vladislav's body.

The old man's wife, Babcia, silently vowed to return with shovels and competent diggers. When the permafrost had softened, she would give her husband a proper burial. That was the least she could do for him, a man so selfless and stubborn as to starve so that others could eat.

But for now, she must concentrate on the living: her daughter, worn out from grief and from tending to the village cows, and her grandsons, who were too small to be doing such difficult, sad work, but too young to leave behind.

I REMEMBER HOW difficult this burial was for all of us. Physically taxing, emotionally draining, we suffered a great deal. Mother and Grandmother especially struggled with granting my grandfather's wishes, but ultimately, they listened and honored them, even when his wishes were painful for them to fulfill.

One of our most important human skills is the ability to listen—*really* listen—to those around us. Being an active, empathetic listener is not easy. Psychotherapists and counselors spend a lot of time developing this skill. In order to get into a deep listening experience, we must be quite secure personally. In the process of listening, we open ourselves to be influenced. Some of our beliefs may be threatened, and we may become vulnerable. In a sense, it's a paradox: in order to *have* influence you must allow yourself to *be* influenced.

To emphasize this point, I will reference "John," a young teenage boy with whom I worked for many sessions. At the time of his initial referral, John was presented to me as the rebellious son of successful, professional parents. His unacceptable behavior included stealing, drug use, expulsion from school for fighting, and even physical violence against his father. Initially, I felt a great deal of sympathy for John's parents. They were obviously dealing with a stubborn, difficult child.

After several sessions of active listening however, during which I expended a great deal of effort to suspend my own personal judgment, my understanding of the situation changed dramatically. I gained a great deal of empathy and admiration for John, who turned out to be a bright young man simply attempting to survive in a situation where he was not loved or appreciated. He was also living under an inflexible system, designed by his parents, to control his every move.

I came to believe that John's acting-out behavior was a desperate attempt to establish his individuality and salvage his own sanity. Follow-up interviews with John's parents confirmed my initial understanding of the situation. Eventually, by mutual agreement, and after many sessions, his removal from that home was the beginning of healing for John.

By listening intently, and suspending my own judgment (as a father myself, I could easily have sided with the beleaguered parents), I was able to look beyond the obvious and truly hear how best to help John, even when it flew in the face of conventional wisdom.

Truly listening to those who are unsettled—attempting to understand, suspending judgment—sometimes results in the uncomfortable realization that there can be very little difference between the so-called "insane" and the so-called "sane" among us. There is a running joke among psychotherapists that goes something like this:

Therapist: "So, Mrs. So-and-so, I understand that
   several members of your family suffer from mental
   illness."
Patient: "Oh, no, doctor. They don't suffer."
Therapist: "They don't?"
Patient: "No. They quite enjoy it."

The hidden meaning of the joke is that we all suffer from some degree of mental dysfunction, but how we cope with it determines how we are viewed by society.

The greatest obstacle to intensive listening is resistance on the part of the listener, particularly when we are asked to understand those who threaten our firmly held beliefs, whose lives may be very different from our own, or even those whom we perceive as a threat to our own safety or way of life. If you truly understand your enemy, he will no longer be your enemy. You will not hate him, you will not be driven to destroy him, and you will become vulnerable.

Ironically, this very obstacle that can be so difficult to surmount is the only obstacle over which we have complete control. No one else can remove that stubborn obstacle but you. You must open your ears to the words and open your heart to understanding. And to truly listen, to truly understand what another person is saying, you must go along to that vulnerable place and meet the other person there.

ONE WEEK AFTER Vladislav's death, Babcia awoke from a dream with a sudden start. She sat up, gasping, from her mat on the floor. In the dream, her dead husband had come to her. At first, as she rubbed the sleep from her eyes and checked to see that the children still slept, she worried that her mind was going. She was old, grieving the loss of her husband, there was never enough food to keep from starving or fuel to keep from freezing, and there were children and grandchildren to worry about and protect. Perhaps it was all too much.

But as she thought about the dream, in the quiet of the hut with her daughter and grandsons asleep on the floor around her, it became more real, not less. Vladislav *had* stood before her in his old suit shirt and woolen cloak. With kindness in his eyes but with a fierce determination, he had told her she must get dressed right away. She must walk into the steppe.

"There is a spot where wild strawberries grow in spring," he told her in the dream. "The child, Andrew, knows this place. You must walk there. From that spot, turn to the south, and count out five hundred steps."

The dreaming Babcia interrupted. "But why, my husband? What is there?"

"You will know," he said. "Trust me. Go, and take the child with you."

And so Babcia roused the small child, gently shaking him awake and putting a finger to her lips. "Shh," she said quietly. "Do not wake the others. You must get dressed and come with me."

The small boy knew to obey his grandmother; he dressed

quietly and put on his coat. "Where are we going?" he asked in a whisper, once they were outside. The vast land stretching before them was dark and still. The sun had yet to rise.

"To the strawberry patch. Your Dziadek has told me to go there. He said you must show me. Now hush. I cannot tell you more."

After walking in the cold for what felt like forever, the old woman and the young boy found the now barren patch of strawberries.

"Here, Grandma," said the young child, holding his hand toward a clump of brown and crumpled leaves.

Babcia nodded and turned right. Her face reflected her determination as she took herself back to the dream and her husband's words. She stepped with long strides, counting in Polish as she walked. The boy hurried beside her, two steps to each one of hers.

Before she reached the count of 500, Babcia saw ahead of her a large object on the ground, steaming in the cold morning air. She walked faster, no longer counting. This was what her husband had sent her to find, she was sure of it!

As they neared the object, she could see it was a young calf with its throat torn open by wolves. The kill was fresh. The body was otherwise unmarked. She looked all around at the steppe that surrounded her. There were no wolves in sight.

Babcia smiled. "Thank you, my husband," she said to the air. To her grandson, she said, "Come, Andy. We must drag this home. Tonight we will have meat."

~~~

DID MY GRANDMOTHER receive a visit from my deceased grandfather on that frozen winter night? Or had her subconscious desperately supplied details that offered an alternative to starvation? Six decades later there is no way to say with certainty, but I *can* tell you this: My grandmother listened to the details of her dream. She was receptive to the possibilities that presented themselves, and she followed her intuition. Because of that, I am alive today.

Most of the time, we do not listen completely to the words of others. In fact, I believe there are at least four different levels of listening. Sometimes we *pretend to be listening*. We nod our heads and say, "Uh-huh," while actually thinking of something else. We make eye contact but little or nothing of what is being said actually registers.

Selective listening occurs when we interrupt our own thinking long enough to attend to some of the key statements of the other person. We have a rough idea of what the other person is talking about, but not full comprehension.

Attentive listening occurs when we make a real effort to hear and listen to what the other person is saying. We are present and although we may miss some of what is said, most of it is heard and processed and we respond appropriately.

Empathetic listening is the highest level of listening and is done with a total intention to understand the other person without judgment and, most important, without agreeing or disagreeing with what is being said.

As a psychotherapist, I have learned to listen with intensity. Such listening requires absolute attention and total focus. (Perhaps this is why most therapy sessions don't exceed one hour—too exhausting!) There is nothing passive about intensive listening. Only through intensive, empathetic listening can we learn to completely understand the words of our fellow humans—and our fellow humans have a great, burning need to be understood. This is especially true of someone who is suffering.

I should mention here that there is a great difference between *listening* and *hearing*. I can hear what another person is saying and even repeat it back—like a parrot!—without really having understood the words at all. True listening includes an understanding of what has been said.

Under normal conditions, when another person speaks, our minds are actively formulating a response based on whether we agree or disagree. As the playwright Albert Guinon said, "There are people who, instead of listening to what is being said to them, are already listening to what they are going to say themselves."

How do we move beyond merely hearing, to active, empathetic listening? I have found the following tips useful.

Establish eye contact. This sounds simple, but it is also the most often ignored piece of advice. Look at the other person when she speaks to you. Don't look around the room. Don't glance away repeatedly. Don't busy yourself with some other task. Look her in the eye and you will show her that you care and that you are *there* and not off somewhere else in your mind.

Pay attention to nonverbal cues. What a person says without words—the way he crosses his arms over his chest, wrinkles his brow, or sighs—tells you at least as much as the words coming out of his mouth. Gestures never lie. If he says, "I am happy," but his shoulders slump, his face droops, and he presses his temples, there are other messages being expressed that need exploring.

Don't judge. The only way to truly understand another person is to suspend judgment. Think of this as a temporary suspension, if necessary. You can always revisit the conversation later and judge all you want. But at this moment, you are doing something important for another human being. You are trying to understand him, and your nonjudgmental understanding is what he most needs.

Ask questions. Avoid direct questions that have only one-word answers. Questions such as, "Do you like your job?" will not serve to further discussion. Open-ended questions, by contrast, are useful in getting a person to talk. Open-ended questions cannot be answered by a simple yes or no, or by a one-word answer. An example of an open-ended question is, "What would be your ideal outcome?" (Be careful not to ask too many questions, though, as this may cause the person to feel as if you are simply being nosy. Too many questions can actually make an individual shut down.) I have found that the most effective use of a question is as a way to end a long silence.

Initiate touch. There is something magical about a gentle human touch—nonaggressive, undemanding, and nonsexual. A touch of the hand communicates, "I care," "I am here for you." In many situations, it is better than anything you can say. And it can be the best thing when you are at a loss for words. A simple hug has an amazing power to comfort and calm. The need and longing for human touch is innate; we suffer when deprived of it, just as we suffer when deprived of food and water.

The most famous hugger of them all was Leo Buscaglia, who wrote a great deal about the importance of giving and receiving love. He took his message around the world, lecturing to large crowds. When he came to Niagara Falls in the 1970s, I stood in a long line of people waiting to get a hug from Leo. It was worth waiting an hour.

Recognize emotions. In empathetic listening, the intent is to understand not just the ideas being expressed but also the emotions behind them. This is the most important part of feeling understood. I knew I was doing a good job when a woman I'll call Angela, a new patient, with whom I'd only been working for a few months, told me, "I've seen so many therapists in the past ten years. You are the first one who understands me."

Was I some new breed of amazing therapist? No, of course not. I was simply an empathetic listener who paid attention to what she was saying. And this is not a mysterious talent that takes a PhD to obtain. It is an ability you have within yourself, an ability we all have that can be developed and strengthened to great effect.

Intense listening requires that you listen with your body, your eyes, and your heart. But understanding the other person is only half the job. The other, more difficult, half is communicating that understanding so that the other person *feels* understood. Conveying that you *understand* earns you the trust of others, makes people more open to your ideas, and makes them feel more calm and confident. Once you have reached the level where another person feels understood, many things are possible.

4.

_____

Showing Understanding
Is the Greatest Gift

It is well to give when asked, but it is better to give
unasked, through understanding.

—KAHLIL GIBRAN

TWO WEEKS AFTER burying Vladislav, one week after
Babcia's dream that had brought them to the slain calf, the
weather broke. The hours of sunlight lengthened, the birds
called to one another again, and Babcia believed that the
ground had softened enough to return to Vladislav's grave.
They would return and dig a deeper hole so that her husband might have a more suitable final resting place.

The commissar, who was not usually a generous man,
knew that the dead deserved respect—especially a man
like Vladislav, who had died so that others might live. Such
an honorable death must not be disrespected by the living
left behind. The commissar was also a superstitious man.

He did not want to be responsible for bringing the evil eye upon his household, and although he would not admit it, he feared Babcia and her wise old eyes. So he allowed the family to borrow a pair of shovels for the women and two spades for the children from the communal garden's tool supply.

Babcia, her daughter Zosia, and the children set out early in the morning. The women walked, carrying the shovels over their shoulders. The younger child carried both spades, tapping them together each time he took a step, and the older child carried a flattened rock on which the family had taken turns scratching the shape of a cross. This would serve as the old man's headstone.

Beyond the compound of mud huts, beyond the endless flat tundra, at the far edge of the horizon, the sun rose and the day seemed full of good omens. The journey was a serious one, yes, but each family member understood that they would be doing the right thing, giving the old man a better resting place. Plus, the weather was warming, the days were lengthening, the sun shone on the hoarfrost so that the ground sparkled, and for a week the family had eaten meat and soup and marrow from the slain calf.

The children's spirits were high and the day felt hopeful despite the grim purpose of the journey. The boys marched side-by-side and sang. The women did not rein them in; they understood that the children had suffered much and even on this sad, purposeful walk, they smiled to see them happy.

AT A TIME when my grandmother and mother were extremely vulnerable, they made a conscious choice not to lecture my brother and me on our inappropriate behavior that day, but chose instead to understand the pain and hardship we had all been suffering and recognize that we needed the chance to feel good and happy, even on a day that was especially serious for the adults.

"To know someone here or there," wrote Goethe, "with whom you can feel there is understanding in spite of distances or thoughts expressed, that can make life a garden." When we offer the gift of understanding to another, we build a bridge—a bridge that makes all manner of things possible. So actively listening with the intent of understanding another human being becomes a generous act, and—if the person is very different from you—an act that can require a bit of extra work.

I was once assigned a patient I'll call Nancy, who had been living in an institution for chronic mental patients for more than twenty years. She was generally incoherent and had long ago been placed in a "back ward"—the place for hopeless patients who had not responded to any form of therapy and who no longer received the sort of attention given to those patients who still showed the possibility of improvement.

I decided I would counsel Nancy for an hour every day, just to see if any progress could be made. From the beginning, she was very difficult to work with; the majority of what she said during our sessions did not make sense. There was little in the way of speech that I could latch on to, and to make matters worse, she was prone to frequent unprovoked and intensely angry outbursts. It was her unmanageable and disruptive behavior that made no one else want to work with her.

Each day that Nancy and I met, I focused heavily on active listening. I did not judge anything she said but listened as intently as I could and communicated back to her how well I heard what she said. During the first few days, only about 10 percent of what she said made any sense whatsoever. When she said something decipherable, such as, "My sister was a waitress," I would respond with strong interest. ("Did I hear you correctly, Nancy? Your sister worked as a waitress? That's very interesting. Tell me more about her.") Within a few days, Nancy's verbalizations began to make more and more sense. It turned out that she was starved for attention and thrived on someone just listening to her. Really, listening!

Within a month of beginning these sessions, 75 percent of what Nancy talked about made sense, and she continued making progress in her treatment. Eventually, she was able to leave the back ward, move to in-home care, and become a more active participant in her own life. In looking back, I can see that it was simply intensive listening that resulted in the initial breakthrough.

There is a simple, ancient directive that we can all follow in our interactions with others: *Primum non nocere.* "First, do no harm." This is an especially critical insight for couples or families who seek counseling together. Recognizing how much pain and suffering we are causing others is the first step in stopping the pain on all sides. I believe that the very best way we human beings can help each other is simply to stop hurting each other.

In my work with teenagers and couples, the most frequent complaint I hear is, "My parents don't understand me." Or, "My husband (or wife) doesn't understand." A lack of understanding between two parties is clearly the greatest obstacle we face in forming lasting, meaningful relationships. It is also one of the easiest aspects of any relationship to improve.

The simplest and best way to show your understanding is by using a technique I call mirroring—reflecting back the emotion that you hear expressed. Phrases such as "You sound frustrated," or "You must be really angry," or "How upsetting that must have been," are good examples of mirroring. Be sure, though, to use whatever words feel natural to you and try to avoid any hint of "psychobabble," as this can get in the way of your message of understanding.

Don't worry too much about getting the emotion wrong. If you have incorrectly assessed the situation, your friend will correct you and you will have a better understanding. If you *are* correct, simply hearing you restate his emotion will lift a huge weight from his psyche.

Remember, too, that words alone cannot convey the full spectrum of human communication. As Elbert Hubbard wrote, "He who does not understand your silence will probably not understand your words." If we are truly to understand one another, we must not only understand the words being said but also the emotions being expressed. How can we do this? Remember those *nonverbal cues* discussed in Chapter Three? Well, this is your chance to pay closer attention to those slumped shoulders, to that weary rubbing of the temples.

Each time we interact with others we are presented with body language clues. Many of the commonplace signals have become clichéd: the drumming of fingers to show impatience, stroking the chin to signify deep thought, biting fingernails to express worry, and rubbing hands in anticipation are a few examples of familiar body language. But it is important to understand that these are not merely clichés, they are real, specific forms of communication that are either inborn (even blind babies smile) or learned through a lifetime of complex social interactions and observations. If we are alert, and pay attention to such indirect communiqués, they will help us to understand others at an even deeper level than attentive listening can provide.

Of prime importance, also, is the realization that it is possible to understand *how* another person feels, without approving or disapproving of those feelings. Not everything a suffering person says will make sense to you. You will not always agree that their emotional reactions are valid for the situation, and some things you hear may even be extremely unsettling. But the greatest gift you can give to other human beings is the simple gift of understanding what *they* are feeling and what they are going through at a given moment.

Regular, active, attentive listening brings us closer to understanding others at the most basic level, and this understanding serves to enhance all of our relationships. Whether between a parent and child, a boss and employee, a patient and counselor, or a husband and wife, any conscious attempt to understand the other person breaks down barriers. It engenders trust, lowers tension, clears up misunderstandings, and opens the way for deeper, richer, more satisfying relationships.

BABCIA AND ZOSIA stopped and shielded their eyes from the intense sunlight. Behind them, the children also stopped, awaiting instructions. The two women scanned the horizon before them, searching for the mound of earth and stones that had been the final resting place of the husband of one and the father of the other. They felt that they must surely be in the correct spot, but even looking in every direction, they could not locate the small mound of earth that would signify the shallow grave.

It was the child, Andrew, who first saw the scattered stones. "There, Mama," he cried, pointing, and the family advanced. As they drew nearer, they could see that there were many stones scattered about. There was also a slight depression in the earth surrounded by a bit of loosened soil.

In silent agreement, the four family members began to walk in circles, head down, canvassing the surrounding area for clues. Soon enough, drag marks were located and followed. They led the family to an unfortunate discovery: the scattered fragments of a human being. Their worst fears had been confirmed. The starving wolves had taken Vladislav's remains and pulled them from the earth. They had eaten what was left of the young child's grandfather, the young woman's father, the old woman's husband.

The sight of a clump of her father's hair seemed to be more than the young woman could bear. She broke down in a way she had not before, not even during the worst of the banishment and the suffering that had followed. Although she tried to hold them back, her tears turned into great, heaving sobs. Her children and her mother stepped forward to touch and comfort her. After the sobs subsided, the family reburied the remains that they could find, placed the carved stone they had brought, gathered their tools, and began the long walk home.

As they walked in silence, Babcia was reminded of her dream, of how her husband had come to her while she slept and how what he told her led them to a calf, slain by wolves. With each step she began to reframe her thinking, to search for understanding.

Her husband's body had fed the wolves—a sad, painful fact. And yet the wolves had fed her family in return; they had slain a calf and left it on the steppe and it had fed her family for a week. The calf's throat had been torn, but the meat left otherwise untouched. Babcia had never known wolves to act in such a strange way. It was very odd behavior.

Could it be that some part of her husband's fierce protective nature had remained behind with the wolves to keep watch over the family? Was there some part of her own dear Vladislav that was now also part wolf?

EVER SINCE THAT sad, painful day on the plain, my grandfather has been inextricably linked in my mind with wolves. There is a sadness, yes, but also a sense of circularity. I have learned a lot about wolves over the years. I have donated to charities that protect them and have kept a special fondness for them in my heart.

Most people—if they think of wolves at all—think of the "lone wolf" silhouetted on a ridgeline, howling at the moon. That is one way to imagine wolves, certainly. But it is not a complete view. Wolves are also very family oriented, fiercely loyal, and they work together as a pack to raise the young, hunt, and bring in food for all to eat.

With greater understanding, I have developed an extraordinary fondness for wolves as well as compassion for their plight—creatures living by their wits on the fringes of land that unfortunately often overlap with human ranchlands. The life of a wolf is not easy.

When we actively seek understanding, as I have done with the wolves, we remove the barriers of fear and foreignness. Without fear and foreignness, we are better able to appreciate and help others. It was Nietzsche who said, "What else is love but understanding and rejoicing in the fact that another person lives, acts, and experiences otherwise than we do?"

Understanding can take many forms.

In the 1970s, a patient I was working with at the time helped me to find understanding on a whole new level. During our sessions, "Marcus" used to talk about seeing auras (human energy fields that some see as a colorful light surrounding a person). I have never been able to see auras, and so I remained skeptical. I wanted to believe that Marcus saw the auras he claimed to, but like most people, I often find it difficult to believe what I cannot see.

I had long been familiar with the concept of personal energy fields, of the fact that each of us has a scientifically verifiable, measurable magnetic field surrounding us, an electrical charge resulting from the many complex chemical processes going on within us at all times, but I had not accepted the notion of auras. The notion intrigued me, though, and I decided to run my own experiment.

On a morning when I was scheduled to counsel Marcus, I took time before work to practice a specific meditation. Marcus was the first patient I would see that morning, and in my meditation I spent time visualizing myself surrounded by a violet flame.

The moment Marcus entered my office, he exclaimed with great surprise, "Oh, wow! I have never seen a violet aura before in my life! That's beautiful!"

My little experiment led me to understand that he truly could see what I could not.

And, contrary to popular belief, the aura is not a New Age idea. Since the beginning of time, spiritual beings have been depicted surrounded by various fields of energy. If you accept the notion of the saint with his halo of light, you are accepting the notion of an aura. And everyone is familiar with the angry person depicted with a black storm cloud that follows him wherever he goes. This is another (albeit cartoonish) image that may help you to imagine how an aura might exist and how it might appear.

The energy each one of us produces can influence others in positive or negative ways. Think about it. If you sit for an extended period next to a person who is angry or depressed, you will often begin to feel the same emotions. Similarly, if you sit next to a person who is relaxed, peaceful, and positive, you will also be affected by his or her state.

This is one reason it is so important that we focus on our own inner state when attempting to reach out to others. And if we focus on being calm and relaxed—taking the time to really listen and search for understanding—important things that are not outwardly obvious can become clear and real, leading us to be more effective, empathetic, and compassionate in all our interactions.

When Adlai Stevenson said, "Understanding human needs is half the job of meeting them," he was probably referring to physical needs, but I believe his words apply equally to the emotional needs of humans. Once we understand *what* someone's emotional needs are, we are more than halfway there. And if we can then convey that understanding—really communicate that we understand—we have touched another person and extended a ray of hope. And hope is an emotion that can see you through the toughest of times.

5.

Hope Can See You Through the Toughest Times

> Hope is the thing with feathers
> That perches in the soul.
> And sings the tune, without the words,
> And never stops at all.
>
> —EMILY DICKINSON

AFTER HER HUSBAND'S death, Babcia knew that she would need to find some means of feeding her family if they were to survive their time in Siberia. When they arrived, her daughter Zosia, young and strong, had been assigned to mix the clay for building mud huts; later she was put to work herding the cows of the "Solholz," the Communist Collective to which they had been assigned. As payment for Zosia's daily backbreaking work, the family received one 2-pound loaf of bread a week.

Babcia knew they would need more food than that to survive as a family. But she was much older than her daughter. She was not physically strong; she could not work in the fields. So Babcia decided that if she was to help feed her family, she must find a way to use her mind to get them food.

One day, over a game of cards with her grandsons, Babcia had trouble concentrating. An idea was growing in her head as she stared at the cards in her hand.

"Grandmother," said the youngest, "it is your turn."

Babcia looked down at the cards in her hands. She studied the bright colors. A deck of cards had been the only diversion small and light enough to bring with the family when they fled their earlier, much different life. Vladislav had insisted that the small space the cards would occupy in the suitcase of essentials would be worth it in the long run. He knew that the opportunity for diversion could be as important as food in surviving an extended hardship. Babcia took out the queen of diamonds. She turned it over and over as she thought.

"Grandmother?"

"I will be a fortune teller," she said suddenly. And for the remainder of that afternoon, Babcia practiced laying the cards out in lines and telling the fortunes of her daughter and her grandsons until she could make a fortune from the cards without hesitation.

Perhaps it was the bleak countryside, or the long, sunless winter days that made the villagers crave a glimpse of a better, brighter future. Perhaps it was their Eastern European upbringing, steeped as it was in superstition and myth. Whatever the reason, the villagers came to Babcia to hear their fortunes. And Babcia, when she foretold their lives, always tried to give them hope. What was the sense of spreading more suffering with bad predictions? No, Babcia believed in hope.

Soon she was visiting the more prosperous people of the village and using her cards to tell them the fine qualities that they possessed, or even what they might need to work on to be better people. If a little good could come of it—if, because of her fortune telling, an angry neighbor stopped hitting his wife, or a mother stopped calling her daughter ugly—well, what was the harm in that?

Often, in exchange for their fortunes, the villagers would give Babcia a carrot, a potato, or a piece of bread. In this way she helped to keep her family alive.

MY GRANDMOTHER BELIEVED in hope and transmitted that belief to all of us. As children, my brother and I learned that no matter how many things we might lose, hope was something that could never be taken from us. And as long as hope is kept alive, it can be fed and nurtured until it grows stronger than despair. I know this from my years of clinical practice, and I know this from experience.

Hope is not an elusive trait that is only granted to a fortunate few. It is a personal power that we all have the ability to possess. It is always there for the taking. Even in the bleakest circumstances, if we can find but a small spark of hope, we can nurture it, feed it until it becomes a great fire of determination. As my family did, in Siberia.

The great Roman orator Cicero summed up this idea simply and succinctly when he coined the saying, "Where there's life, there's hope."

I once had a patient I'll call Daniel, who had been admitted to a mental hospital in the 1950s and had been a patient for more than twenty years. He had lost any hope of ever "getting out." (In that era, getting *into* a psychiatric hospital was easy; getting *out* was hard.) I was assigned to Daniel's case, and we quickly developed a good working relationship. I soon discovered that he was an amiable fellow, with no compelling reason to remain institutionalized. After twenty years, however, Daniel was terrified at the thought of leaving. His extended stay had become comfortable, whereas the outside world represented the uncomfortable, a frightening unknown.

My job, thereafter, became making Daniel *want* to leave. The first thing I did was to obtain permission to take him out once a week as part of his therapy. At first, he was terrified by a world that had changed drastically since his last experience of it, in the 1950s. But gradually he began to enjoy our walks in the park, our lunches in a restaurant, trips to the zoo, the grocery store, traveling on a city bus. And before long, Daniel developed a real desire to go on our outings and a real sense of hope for a new life. Ultimately, this simple act of reestablishing hope led to his release and resumption of a normal life. I like to call this my "Here's what you're missing" approach.

Hope and happiness go hand in hand. Hopeful people are happier people. They are more resilient, more purposeful, have better self-esteem, and even take better care of themselves. My family lived this credo and I believe it to this day.

In the years since Siberia, I've come to see my grandmother's fortune-telling as an example of her resourcefulness and hope for our future. Even in the midst of a situation that most would find hopeless, she found a way to help her family and to offer hope to others. She encouraged us to believe in ourselves, and showed us by her example that we need never give up. She taught us the value of nurturing our own unique strengths as a means to help ourselves and also to help others. She would not give up, so none of us did.

Most of the residents of that small Siberian village spoke as if Siberia were the end of the line. They had no hope of leaving, and, as a result, most did not leave. My family, however, spoke every day of a time when we could leave Siberia. We believed in it. We nurtured that belief, and it gave us hope.

What do you believe in? What generates your outlook on life? Your actions on behalf of others? Examine this idea for a moment, if you will, because *why* you reach out to others is directly related to how effective you will be. Helping can be engendered by many positive emotions: gratitude, love, and compassion are just a few. But not all helping is generated by pure motives.

Some people help others because they want a reward, even if it is the far distant reward of earning a place in heaven, of currying God's favor. Such a person may not make an outward show of helping others, but still she wants every good deed tallied into the book of judgment. In fact, she may console herself in private with her many good deeds as proof that she is a virtuous person.

Some people help others so that they will earn a good place in their community. This is the person who is always telling you just how many "good works" he has done, how altruistic he is. This person wants his plaque on the wall saying just how much good he has done or how much money he has donated to help the needy.

Some people help out of a sense of duty. Because this person has been told that helping is what a good person does, because she has been told to, been taught to, she does it. Chances are she performs it as a duty, something to check off the list of what *should be done.* Chances are also good that her "helping" does not really do herself or others much good because it is done by rote, not by spirit.

Who you are, what is at the core of you, what beliefs and hopes inspire you, these will be the driving forces that give you the energy to help others. Helping that comes out of more selfish motives is likely to produce less genuine results. Sometimes, such helping can even produce more harm than good. People who engage in helping for selfish reasons are often referred to as "do-gooders."

Instead of being do-gooders, who force our own agendas on others, we must look to the individual to understand what that person most needs and also what we are best able to provide.

A good friend of mine is now unable to leave her house. Mary is not well. I make it a point to talk to her on the phone at least twice a week. These phone conversations have become very important to her. Calling Mary is truly a small thing, but because she is housebound, the calls have become her lifeline to the outside world, her connection to a friend, her hope. We recently talked about this and she said to me, "Put that in your book, Andy." And so I am. For you, Mary.

ZOSIA WAS GRATEFUL to be alive and grateful she had not been separated from her mother and her children, but she did not care for this new life in Siberia. Living in a wasteland was hard, made more stressful by the appalling lack of food and also fuel for warmth. She missed her former life in Poland; there she had been young and popular—even privileged. And even more than Poland, she missed her husband and longed to see him again. She worried every day how he was faring in the Russian prisoner-of-war camp.

In her earlier life in Lvov, Poland, Zosia had often wondered where she would find the time to accomplish everything that needed doing each day. In Siberia, she wondered how she would fill the long hours of cold and darkness. She missed music and dancing and motorcars in the streets. She missed novels and the theater. She missed dinner parties with friends and servants to help with daily chores. Nothing was the same in Siberia, nothing.

But Zosia did not complain to her family. Instead, she looked for the good, the beautiful, the inspiring, every day believing that a spark of hope could light a fire that would someday set them free. She knew her children and her mother suffered. The long hours without adequate food stretched to days and weeks and finally years. Seeing her children starving made

Zosia feel more helpless than she had ever felt. And beyond the hunger, each family member struggled to accept the stillness and quiet of the long winter nights, the interminable stretches of time with nothing to occupy them but the hunger in their stomachs and the thoughts within their heads.

So Zosia strived to appreciate the wonders of small things. She tried every day to pass that appreciation on to her two young children.

"Andrew, Jurek, come quickly," she might call, and the children would rush to her side.

"Do you see this?" Their mother would sigh, indicating the vast red-violet glow of a sunset that spread across the plain right up to the door of their hut. "Isn't it beautiful?"

Or the time when young Andrew had asked his mother why the sky was sparking with fire and so the family stood in the cold, staring at the northern lights with mouths agape. "This is how I know God is with us," Zosia said, pulling her young sons close. "He has not left us. That is hope that you see. Hope, lighting up the sky."

Even a colorful butterfly flitting past, the discovery of a delicious mushroom, a handful of wild strawberries, or the beauty of a spider's web covered with morning dew was a cause for gratitude in Siberia. It was a chance to celebrate the beauty of life, of nature, a reminder that there was still good in the world.

In these small ways, Zosia learned to find encouragement, the will to continue, the will to survive. She cultivated hope from everyday wonders and it gave her faith in the rightness of the world, hope to see her through a time of great suffering. Zosia's hope and enthusiasm were contagious. She shared them freely and they helped to keep her family alive.

In Siberia, my mother had the courage to cultivate hope where others found none. She learned to slow down and appreciate each day for the small pleasures that it brought. The beauty and promise of the world that she called to our attention helped us to understand the unselfish nature of gratitude. We learned to be grateful for any blessing, no matter how small. That openness of spirit fed our hope— hope that we would someday return to the life we had known before.

My mother's hope was also a precious part of what kept us all alive. "In the midst of winter, I found there was, within me, an invincible summer," wrote Camus. His words speak so eloquently to my family's time in Siberia. Yes, the cold winters were overwhelming, but we refused to let the winter inside our hearts. We kept the warm rays of hope alive and they, in turn, kept us alive.

In the 1970s, a young woman came to me as a patient. "Martha" had been raised in a very strict, fundamentalist home and her upbringing had so restricted her actions and thoughts that she had no sense of herself remaining. Our paths crossed after Martha was hospitalized for attempting suicide. In an environment that allowed for no personal choices and no freedom of expression, Martha had come to believe that she had no chance for growth and therefore nothing to live for.

In our initial therapy sessions, Martha replied to my questions in a flat monotone, using as few words as possible. Her shoulders slumped and she would not meet my gaze. I knew we had a long way to go. What surprised me, though, was how quickly Martha responded to the simplest of treatments. I began by asking her what, as a child, she had dreamed of growing up to be. At first she told me that she hadn't had any dreams, but the more we talked the more it became clear that she had—doesn't every child?—but that her adult influences had discouraged her from even a hope of fulfilling those dreams.

Once Martha opened up and trusted me with her hopes and dreams, we laid out a plan to achieve them, and her improvement was dramatic. The light came back into her eyes and soon she was bringing suggestions to me to discuss. Martha began to speak easily of what she someday hoped to accomplish. Shortly after completing her treatment, Martha moved away to pursue her future, but I can say with certainty that the one simple change in how she viewed her possibilities was enough to turn everything else in her life around.

"I know how men in exile feed on dreams of hope," wrote Aeschylus in his famous play *Agamemnon*. It was true in the fourth century B.C.E., it was true for us in Siberia, and it is still true today. Hope can see you through the toughest times.

Fortunately, hope is a skill that we can all learn to cultivate. And like gratitude, it tends to be self-perpetuating. If you are more hopeful, you are more resilient, trusting, and open, traits that allow you to receive good things from the world, which in turn increases your hopefulness. A delicious circle.

And yet, in my work with patients, I often encounter a deliberate roadblock to hope. In a discussion of the subject, a client might tell me, "But I don't want to have *false* hope." I've heard that sentiment expressed a lot, but over the years I have come to believe that *false hope* is a misnomer. Hope is a belief, a virtue, akin to faith, charity, gratitude, even patience. We do not say false faith, false gratitude, false patience. That does not make sense. Likewise, there is no such thing as false hope. What people refer to as false hope is what I would call *denial*. Denial is refusing to see the reality of a situation—denying its truth. A person in denial is inflexible.

A hopeful person, by contrast, is neither delusional nor inflexible. A hopeful person sees reality and makes a conscious choice to view potential outcomes in the best possible light. Hopeful people have specific goals with several acceptable outcomes in mind, and a backup plan for achieving them.

There is always room for hope.

According to Greek myth, Pandora opened a forbidden box that contained all the world's evils. When she lifted the lid to peek inside, the evils escaped. Pandora slammed the lid shut just as Hope, who was slower, was also trying to emerge, trapping it inside the box. The world had been a blissful paradise before Pandora's box was opened. Afterward, suffering, disease, and death plagued the land. Not until Pandora finally returned to the box and freed Hope did humanity find a way to survive suffering. Hope, we learn, is stronger than the evils of the world.

And yet, as strong as hope is, it is merely the genesis. Hope provides the impetus that leads the call to action. And when hope fuels our actions, those actions are far more likely to be successful. Continuing to hope in the face of adversity, despite many obstacles that would derail us, is what we have come to call *perseverance*. And perseverance is what gives "teeth" to hope.

6.

___

Perseverance: The "Teeth" of Hope

Living calls for the art of the wrestler, not the dancer.
Staying on your feet is all; there is no need
for pretty steps.

—MARCUS AURELIUS

ZOSIA ROSE EARLY, as she did every morning, and left the hut before sunrise. The air was biting-cold, and she pulled her cloak more closely around her as she walked to the small corral on the outskirts of the village. Babcia, with her old eyes, may have managed to avoid working, but Zosia had been unable to escape conscription. All able-bodied individuals were expected to assist in maintaining the Communist state.

Zosia's most recent assignment had been to tend the village cows. Many in the village considered this an enviable position; it was not as physically taxing as hoeing the fields from sunup to sundown, nor as messy as making mud-and-straw bricks for building. And at first, Zosia, too, felt that it would be an easy job. For a woman such as herself—a woman who spoke three languages, who read her novels in French, who had graduated from university—what could be so difficult about taking care of cows? She had seen them from afar, grazing in the countryside. She had seen them in the picture books she read to Andrew and Jurek. Cows were quiet and slow. Zosia could certainly tend cows to satisfy the commissar's requirements.

What Zosia had not counted on was how very large cows actually were. When she first entered the barn, the heavy odor of urine and manure nearly overwhelmed her. The cows sighed and shifted their massive bulk, chewing—always chewing—and occasionally lowing piteously. Oh, it made the hairs on the back of her neck stand up. Surely these huge animals would trample her!

To her fellow cattle tenders, Zosia's worry provided a source of great amusement—this cultured woman, this elegant society lady, was afraid of cows. Oddly enough, Zosia did not mind the teasing. It reassured her that she was out of place among the cows, and the light approach comforted her.

Zosia opened the heavy barn door and stepped inside, giving wide berth to a cow that stood nearby, placidly chewing its cud.

"Again you come, the better to be near your beloved cows?" teased Marya, an older Russian woman. Marya's teeth were bad and caused her great pain. She rarely smiled, but her words were gently teasing.

Zosia shuddered as she looked around the barn. "Such brutish creatures. Mannerless and slow."

Marya scooped feed into a wooden trough as she spoke. "You must show them you are in charge, society lady. You must *make* them listen." A dusting of chaff flew into the air with each dump of the scoop.

"They are too big. They are dumb animals. I cannot make them do anything."

Marya laughed and slapped her dusty hands against the front of her dress. "If the cow, she misbehaves, thump her with your knee. She will stop whatever bad thing she is doing."

Zosia shook her head but said nothing. Marya continued. "Your own children have no fear. Your boys were here yesterday. They were petting the cows through the fence. The little one pointed to a cow and said, *dama*. "Lady," he said. And he petted her."

"Yes," said Zosia. "My sons are brave. For me it is brave just to show up for work."

"But you get one loaf of bread each Friday for the honor," said Marya. "The state is generous, no?"

Zosia was not sure if the woman was joking. If so, it was a very risky joke. Even implied frustration could get one in trouble. Such speaking of the mind was not done in Stalin's Russia. The walls had ears. Zosia thought of the family that depended on her and said nothing in reply, but she was silently grateful to Marya for expressing the reality out loud, even if only in the barn. Had she sensed that Zosia would not turn her in? Perhaps the Russian peasant and the society lady were not so different at the bottom of it all.

"Your boys are thin," said Marya. "Too thin."

It was true. Zosia could deny it no longer. Their malnourished bellies protruded beneath a ribcage of which every rib could be counted. Their heads sat too large on skinny necks. Their arms and legs had become impossibly long. Zosia's face burned at the thought and she turned her head away. The peasant woman touched her on the shoulder and whispered, "There is no shame in having nothing when everything has been taken from you. My ancestors, too, were left here three generations ago to starve and die."

Zosia turned to look at Marya. For a moment, there was kindness in the woman's eyes, then, abruptly, she returned to her businesslike manner. "Listen. Next, I will feed the pigs. Their slop? Grains, vegetable peelings—you know they eat better than we do? They do. Maybe tonight when I am feeding them I will forget and leave a bucket by the gate, eh? I am very forgetful these days." Marya winked and clucked her tongue.

Zosia's throat constricted. The barn swam before her eyes. She nodded.

"Remember, no shame," said the woman, and she set about feeding the next row of cows.

BACK IN POLAND, eating slops intended for swine would have been an unthinkable humiliation. In Siberia, we were grateful for them, as they represented a chance for survival. We were starving. We ate anything we could to stay alive.

My mother, a city woman, was very proud, but she learned how to surrender that pride to feed her starving family. Instead of giving up, she persevered, even when it meant she must adapt to things that she would never have accepted before.

She was deathly afraid of the cows she tended. But when the Commissar assigned her that job, she did not refuse. It was not wise to say no to such assignments, and so she was forced to learn to deal with the beasts, and she did. She told herself it was for her children and her mother that she went every day to the barn, and it gave her a focus outside herself. It was a daily choice that she made—a choice to persevere.

Sometimes our success, or even—in the case of my mother

in Siberia—our survival, depends on simply showing up. Being where you are supposed to be, doing what needs to be done is the first step in making good things happen. In my mother's case, she had to tend a herd of cows that terrified her, but the thought of her children starving terrified her more, and so she went, every day, to do the job she had been assigned. She persevered, even though it was unpleasant for her. And she became stronger. Eleanor Roosevelt said, "You must do the things that you cannot do—you gain strength, courage, and confidence by every experience in which you really stop to look fear in the face." She could have penned that sentence for my mother.

Whether you are happy or unhappy is generated by your thoughts and your expectations as well as your determination. "People are just about as happy as they make up their minds to be," Abraham Lincoln said. I remember learning that lesson in Siberia when I experienced many moments of extreme happiness, when I saw a beautiful flower or butterfly, heard a whistled song, saw my mother smile, or ate a piece of bread and chose to see them as gifts. I made a decision to allow them to make me happy. The gifts were small, but they were everywhere, as they are today. The key is to learn to look for them and to be open to them.

Siberia is where I developed my intense love of and respect for nature, which has become a source of great happiness in my life. And to date, some of my most successful efforts to help young people have been on camping trips into the wilderness where individuals are immersed in nature and where they often must battle fatigue and soreness in order to make it to the next campsite. They learn to persevere and in so doing find and recognize a strength they didn't even know they possessed. This can be very empowering.

I also encourage my patients to give gardening a try as a form of therapy. Nurturing vegetables and flowers, watching them grow and bloom and seed is a balm for the soul. If you are a gardener or a camper or a hiker, why not invite the troubled individual you know to join you? You'll be surprised at how beneficial such practical, concrete pursuits can be for them.

Early in my career, I had the opportunity to work with two excellent and very practical counselors. Richard and Becky were effective and competent therapists, the best I have ever encountered when dealing with and helping the chronically mentally ill. They were committed, caring, creative, genuine and a joy to work with. What would likely surprise most people today is that neither one of them had attended college. Most of their skills were practical skills learned "on the job" through perseverance, or were purely intuitive and came from their hearts.

Today we turn to professionals to fix everything. Our loved ones visit psychiatrists, lawyers, clergymen or other specialists, when, in fact, much of what they seek is actually within them if they will but tap into the deep well of human understanding that we all possess. We can help them if we really listen, seek to understand their needs, and give them the support they crave.

After leaving Siberia, I lived in several economically struggling parts of the world (Iran, Palestine, postwar England, Okinawa), and what I noticed in each was that, despite the lack of material possessions, many of the individuals were happy. I mean truly happy. The happiness of these people was generated by their relationships, their work, their activities and spiritual beliefs, and above all by their values. In Okinawa, I spent two years getting to know the locals and I remember fondly the natives that I came to know on the island. As a group, they were without a doubt the happiest and the wisest people I have ever encountered. It was there I learned that what you have in your head and your heart is much more important than what you have in your pocket or in your stomach.

Education provides us with valuable knowledge. When we are educated, we know more and can accomplish more. But what I've learned in seventy-three years of experience is that happiness is not a product of knowledge but a product of wisdom. Many of the people I've met in my life were uneducated, wise, and happy. Homespun philosophers, if you will. There is an old Chinese saying: "To attain knowledge, add something every day; to attain wisdom, remove something every day."

Addressing a person's values and beliefs can contribute more to their happiness than giving them money or physical possessions. The poor often live their lives believing that money will make them happy. Having counseled many very wealthy people who were profoundly unhappy, I disagree. Money can make things easier, certainly, but that does not always translate into happiness and satisfaction. Sometimes I have wished that I could send those wealthy, unhappy people to Siberia for a couple of years—send them to Siberia to teach them the lessons of striving and perseverance, and thereby make them happier.

IT WAS FEBRUARY 1941, nearing the end of the second long winter in Siberia, and the family was weakened by intense hunger. Once again, they found themselves living at the edge of starvation. And once again, Babcia received a visitation from her husband in the form of a dream. This time, Vladislav instructed her to have her daughter Zosia walk several miles to reach a nearby town.

"Wh—" she began.

But again the answer was, "She will understand when she gets there."

After the miracle of the calf, Babcia's instructions to the

family in response to her dreams were not questioned. So Zosia—as hungry and exhausted as she was—donned her cloak and walked to town. She had no idea what she would find, but her mother had assured her she would know what to do when the time came and so she trusted.

Shortly after Zosia entered the gates of the town, an old woman walked up to her. She carried a large sack of flour on her head and behaved as if she knew her.

"This flour is bad," the woman said, directing her gaze solidly at Zosia.

Zosia looked behind her to make sure the woman was not speaking to someone else. There was no one there. "That is unfortunate," she said, turning back to the woman, unsure what her reaction should be.

The old woman pulled the heavy sack down from her head and set it on the ground in front of her body. "You may take it if you want," she said, gesturing with her hands. "I have no use for spoiled flour."

"*How* is it spoiled?" Zosia did not want to lug home a rotten bag of flour if it might make everyone sick.

"The flour is full of weevils," said the woman, pushing the bag toward Zosia with her foot.

Zosia almost laughed. There was a time not so long ago that the thought of weevils in her flour would have disgusted her. She would have thrown it out. But not now.

Weevils, she thought. *Who cares about weevils?* Weevils could be picked out. Weevils could even be cooked in the bread and eaten. Weevils were nothing.

"Well, spoiled flour is better than no flour," said Zosia, pretending to be uncertain, "which is what I have now." She held out her empty hands.

"Yes," said the mysterious woman. She placed the heavy sack into Zosia's arms, turned, and walked back into town.

Zosia was certain she had accomplished what her father had sent her for, and so she, too, turned around and began the long walk home, carrying the precious bag of flour against her hip as she would a baby.

When she arrived back at the hut, Babcia met her at the door.

"You have something." Her mother's eyes were hopeful.

"Flour," said Zosia. "But the woman who gave it to me said it was full of weevils."

"Weevils are nothing. Your father, again, he has provided for us." She crossed herself and raised her eyes heavenward. "Thank you, dear husband."

Zosia lowered the bag onto the floor and rubbed her neck; a sack of flour made for a heavy baby.

Meanwhile, Babcia untied the top of the sack. She would inspect the flour. Even if it proved to be bad, she thought, the heavy burlap sack would still be useful, perhaps as a bed for the youngest child, or a blanket.

When she looked into the opened sack, she let out a cry of surprise.

"Oh," she said, thrusting her hands deep into the white meal. "This flour is fine. It is beautiful. There are no bugs at all!"

I REMEMBER THIS story as one of the miracles that my grandmother liked to tell of our time in Siberia. Just when we had reached the point of absolutely nothing left to eat— on two occasions—a dream about my grandfather led her to food. I don't pretend to know how this worked, but I don't need to know. All I need to be is grateful to my grandmother for never giving up. (And possibly to the spirit of my grandfather, for the same reason!)

My grandmother, a very proud woman, learned some hard lessons about perseverance and practicality while living in Siberia. Those lessons, though difficult, were necessary in order for her to survive and keep her family alive. I am fortunate that she passed those lessons on to me. Hope and perseverance have served me well for over seventy years, and carried me through many adversities. "Every adversity," wrote Napoleon Hill, the best-selling author of *Think and*

Grow Rich, "every failure, every heartache carries with it the seed of an equal or greater benefit."

I vividly remember going into the fields as a child after the wheat harvesters had passed with their scythes. I would carry a small tin cup and pick up all the missed grains I could find, one by one. I spent hours searching for the tiny tan-colored specks lying discarded in the dirt among the stalks and weeds. Talk about perseverance! It was painstaking work, to be sure, but grain by grain, the wheat added up. And when I stopped, I had a small cup of wheat that I could carry home to my family. My mother would boil it up and the grains would expand as they cooked until there were several chewy, nutty mouthfuls for each of us to eat. It made all the work worthwhile and gave us the energy to keep our focus on survival.

Too much of our unhappiness these days is due to the "poor me" syndrome. It's that focus on the self. Mother Teresa was once asked, "If I want to feel better, what should I do?" She responded by saying, "Go out and help someone less fortunate than yourself. It does wonders for the soul."

A patient I'll call Barbara was an extreme example of someone who focused too much on the self. Barbara would complain to anyone who would listen that others were always the cause of her problems. She refused to accept any responsibility for her own life and expected others (including me) to fix her problems for her.

As I do with most of my patients, I gave Barbara homework. She was instructed to focus on ways in which she could help others. I encouraged her to volunteer at her local battered women's shelter, which she did, and Barbara saw very quickly that there were others in the world with much greater need and personal difficulties.

Barbara also learned that an excellent, simple cure for unhappiness is hard work and exercise. Exercise done on a regular basis (three times a week for forty minutes or more) will cause almost anyone to begin to let go of unhappiness. Exercise should always be considered a first, practical approach to rising out of the doldrums. It's been said (and I believe it's true) that if a depressed person digs a hole five feet deep and four feet wide, he will be rid of his depression by the time he is done.

Having a goal to work toward works wonders. Successful people, when asked how they became successful, most often attribute their success simply to being persistent, to refusing to give up. Louis Pasteur, the father of modern microbiology, put it this way: "Let me tell you the secret that has led me to my goal. My strength lies solely in my *tenacity*." Fortunately for the rest of us, Pasteur's persistence did not benefit only him. The discoveries he made so many years ago are still benefiting humanity today and will for decades to come. Thank you, Monsieur Pasteur, for being tenacious, and for having the courage to be yourself.

7.

Find the Courage to Be (Yourself)

By learning to discover and value our ordinariness, we
nurture a friendliness toward ourselves and the world
that is the essence of a healthy soul.

—THOMAS MOORE

THE VILLAGE COMMISSAR, a heavy, sweating man whose
most prominent feature was a cauliflowery wart on his chin,
had the power of life and death over everyone in the village.
He selected villagers to perform specific tasks to keep the
village working and functioning, communist-style. There
were gardens to tend, food to gather and distribute, animals
to supervise and feed, roadwork and construction that must
be done, and he had the power to wave his hand and assign
an individual to a particular job.

Most in the village lived in fear of the commissar, and
none dared to defy his work orders. One day, the commissar
approached Babcia with a determined look on his face. She

knew what he had prepared to say, even before he opened his mouth.

"You will go to work," he said, pointing towards a distant field. Babcia could barely make out the small dark shapes of people stooped over, chopping at the hard earth. "You will take a job in the field, hoeing potatoes. This is your duty to the communist state."

Babcia knew she could not long survive such ill use and at her age would be a poor source of manual labor, besides. She reasoned, in that short space of time, that to die in the fields would be no worse than to die fighting for what was best for her family. She responded to the commissar with a burst of courage.

Babcia pointed her finger at the big man. She stared at him. "In Russia, it is illegal to make old people work. Shame. If you do not give me peace in my old age, I will telegram Stalin. I will telegram Stalin and tell him you have made me to work. You will be very much in trouble."

Even as Babcia said the words, she knew that this greedy, superstitious man had the power to have her thrown into prison, even shot. She could disappear and no one would ever see her again. Her family would starve. She waited a long moment for him to respond, praying that her life would be spared for the sake of her daughter and her grandsons.

The commissar rubbed his wart as if for good luck. He had heard of the old woman's fortune telling. The villagers believed that she was wise, with a powerful eye for the future. A seer's eye.

The commissar stared at Babcia for a long moment. He brought his heavy eyebrows together and frowned in concentration. Then he looked out to the distant field and uttered a loud, "Harrumph!"

He did not order her to work again.

⁓

I AM GRATEFUL, daily, for my grandmother's courage and for the lessons that her courage taught me. At the moments in her life when she had the most fear, she stood up and spoke for what she knew was right.

Having courage does not mean that you are without fear. Courage is what comes when you are afraid but you know you must act anyway. And so you do. Like my grandmother.

Sometimes courage is simply the conscious act of refusing to live in fear. Sometimes it is actively searching for hope in the midst of the most hopeless circumstances imaginable. Sometimes it is finding humor in adversity. I titled this chapter "Find the Courage to *Be*" because I truly believe that it requires great courage to choose to be your most authentic self when others all around you are *acting*, and pretending to be what they think is expected of them.

It also takes courage to *be* in the present moment. So much of what we do involves "futurizing" our time. Where will I go on my next vacation? What will I make for dinner? What should I do with my life? These are important considerations, but we must be careful not to spend *all* of our time thinking about what is yet to come. The future will always be uncertain, but the "now" of our lives *is* certain. It is here and it is now. We are in it.

In Eastern religions, this notion of appreciating the now is called *mindfulness* and it is a state of being that focuses on what we have at this moment. Too many of us forget to "stop and smell the roses," to catch our children being good, to spend a moment really feeling how valuable our friends and family are to us, to smile at our spouses.

Stroking a pet is a simple act of mindfulness—we are thinking of nothing but that animal at that moment in time: the silkiness of the fur, the gratitude for its attention, the warmth of its body. We should take the time to similarly appreciate (and pet!) the humans that we love. To drink in our surroundings, hear the wind in the trees, enjoy the lightning bugs at dusk, linger over a meal, no matter how modest.

In Siberia, we had nothing and so learned to appreciate everything.

Today, we value "being" primarily in terms of action. We like being busy. From childhood, we have been told, "Don't just sit there, do something!" We have been taught that we shouldn't waste time and that the more we accomplish, the better.

When I teach my meditation courses, I begin by writing on the blackboard, "Don't just do something, sit there!" This is, of course, the opposite of what we have been taught since birth.

Because of this cultural emphasis on *doing*, many people use what they do as a way to define themselves, rather than who they *are* as a person. Describing who you are is an interesting exercise to consider. The discussion usually goes something like this:

Me: "Tell me who you are, Bill."

Bill: "I work at a manufacturing plant…"

Me: "No, no. Sorry, not what you *do* for a living. I mean, tell me who you are."

Bill (after a pause): "Well, I have three children—"

Me: "Not what you *have*, Bill. Who you are."

Bill: "Okay, um, I live in—"

Me (insisting): "Who you *are*."

Eventually, a gentle insistence on my part will lead them to a better understanding of the question and a better answer for themselves. It is an important question for all of us to consider, and to consider in the broadest sense. Don't define yourself as a Democrat or a Republican, as a Christian or a Muslim, or even as a man or a woman. Labels are limiting. Instead, try defining yourself by beginning with the words, "I am a human being who is..." and be kind to yourself when finishing the sentence. Never fear—no one else will hear you saying nice things about yourself. No need to be modest. Instead, be honest but gentle: *I am a human being who is kind; I am a human being who is tenacious; I am a human being who is open-minded.*

Another blackboard message I like to use is, "I am not a human *doing*, I am a human *being*." Think about that message for a moment; the truth of it will expand your notion of being.

Meditation, which for many non-Western people is the central event of each day, is essentially "doing nothing." Meditation focuses on a different kind of "being"—of being relaxed, being in the moment, being focused, being peaceful.

Before seeing a patient, I like to focus for a few minutes on being relaxed, caring, and positive, then what I do or say during the session will be generated by my inner state. Offering a textbook response or using an approved technique does not guarantee being a good therapist or a good friend. However, when we concentrate on "being," the words and actions flow in a way that is genuine, spontaneous, effortless, and successful.

THE FAMILY WAS preparing for night when a young Russian soldier opened the door and strode through with an air of officious importance. He did not knock. This was nothing new. Fendrick had visited Vladislav's family many times since their arrival. He believed it was his singular responsibility to instruct them in the ways of the village. And communism. Never did he knock.

"Hello, Old Woman," he said, speaking to Babcia with the tone of teasing disrespect that the two had developed over the months of his visits. To Zosia, he winked and smiled. Zosia was young and attractive, and her beauty was a rare commodity in Siberia, where Russian soldiers often set their sights on the newest female arrivals.

This evening, though, there was a clumsiness to Fendrick's gestures, and he staggered as he approached Babcia. "And how is your God this evening?" he asked. His tone was mocking. Practicing religion was against the law in the communist state; worship was forbidden and Fendrick knew Babcia prayed every day. He had not turned her in, but he knew that she prayed.

Belief in God was Babcia's secret strength; it was the young soldier's secret obsession. He approached her with weaving steps. His breath smelled strongly of alcohol. "Still praying for a miracle?" he asked.

"Not a miracle," said Babcia, gently. "Just a return to Poland."

"Poland," spat out Fendrick. "Your Poland does not miss you. Siberia is home. You do not leave Siberia."

"Thank you, but still I will ask for God to return us to our land—the land we were stolen from, that was stolen from us."

The soldier's face changed. One eye twitched. A vein pulsed in his forehead. He moved across the floor toward Babcia and pulled a gun from his waistband as he walked. Zosia moved as if to protest but a look from her mother kept her silent.

Fendrick held the gun in front of Babcia's face, swaying slightly. Babcia stood very still.

The soldier spoke; his voice was mocking. "Pray now, Old Woman." He pressed the gun to her temple for emphasis. "Pray to your God for help or you will soon be joining him."

Babcia continued to stand very still; the children stared with big eyes. "Our Father, who art in heaven," Babcia began, "hear my prayer."

The soldier cocked his gun.

"Heavenly Father, please bless Fendrick. On this day and on every day, I beseech you to please show Fendrick the healing power of your love."

The soldier looked around the room, confused.

"Fendrick wants to be a good man, Father, he has a good heart. Please show him your love and the path to goodness." He released the hammer from his pistol.

The soldier's eyes glistened. He tucked the gun back into the waistband of his pants. Without another word, he turned and left, leaving Babcia and her family unharmed.

⁓

MY GRANDMOTHER HAD the courage to be who she was, even in the face of threats against her life. She knew what she believed in and she held fast to that. Without aggression or fear, she showed love for the man who threatened her and thereby removed the threat. The soldier could have hurt her, or any one of us, but I believe her courage and conviction were enough to make him turn away and leave us alone.

"Give what you have. To someone, it may be better than you dare think," wrote Henry Wadsworth Longfellow. By this, I think he meant for us to understand that small acts of kindness are as important as elaborate ones, and if we only have a minute, sometimes a minute is all it takes.

We have all heard someone say, "My friend was really there for me. I don't know how I would have gotten through it all without him." Chances are good that the friend did little more than offer a caring and sympathetic ear. It is not what you *do* for people that is so important, or even what you say. It is just being there for them when they need it, when they want to know that they are not alone. It's your presence, your strength and calmness that they most need.

In his book *How Can I Help?* Ram Dass writes, "There's no place special we have to be in order to help out. Right where we are, whatever we're already doing, the opportunity to be of service is almost always present." If we simply stay conscious and aware, we will find an opportunity to give whatever we can to whoever is right there, even if it is something as simple as opening a door for another, or inviting a lonely neighbor to share a meal.

And just as we can never fully comprehend how we have influenced the lives of others, so can we never fully know the continuing impact of our own selfless acts. One act of kindness can create ripples that go on for generations—as my grandfather's did. Even now, his ripples are extending outward to you as you read this book and understand the generosity of his gift, made possible more than sixty years ago, when he gave his life so that I might live. May your understanding of his gift to me inspire you to give to others and in turn inspire others to give. In this way, my grandfather's life and his death may have continued meaning and impact in the world.

"Being present" means being there in the physical sense, but also *being there*, mindfully present, not thinking about what you still have to do at home, not planning what you will wear to an upcoming occasion, but being there with that person who needs you to be there with them.

When I sense that I am not remembering to live in the moment, I have a few tools that I use to *recenter* myself, to balance my emotions and bring my focus back to the here and now. I will often do one or more of these techniques before seeing a patient, or before doing any activity that requires focused attention or active listening.

First, *breathe*. Regular, deep breaths can do wonders for our mental focus and even for our health. As you breathe, really focus on the exchange of oxygen as well as on your breathing and you will quickly be brought back to the present moment. Your focus will sharpen.

Practice being unconditional with yourself. Most often, the time we spend thinking of the past is time we spend judging ourselves: regrets for what we have done or not done, the replaying of scenes and how we might have handled them better, perhaps even thinking of the perfect response days later. Such replaying is a waste of your energy and the opposite of mindfulness.

Attend to your tasks. By focusing intently when performing your daily tasks—even the mundane ones such as shaving or washing the dishes—you can bring yourself back to mindfulness and avoid the rote behaviors that keep us stuck in tired patterns of behavior.

Smile. Nothing picks you up more than a simple smile. Just arranging the muscles of your face into a smile is enough to trigger endorphins that will lift your mood. And, like practiced gratitude, even small smiles lead the way to more and bigger smiles.

Listen. We are surrounded by sounds every day: bird songs, distant trains, music, a breeze through the trees. Take a moment to focus on the sound of what is happening around you and it will bring you back to the present.

Slow Down. Rushing through our days shuts everything out but our own panicked attempts to be at the next meeting on time, or to get the kids to their next after-school event. It elevates blood pressure and causes our stress to skyrocket. Allow yourself a few extra minutes to get where you need to be and the whole trip will be more pleasant.

See something new. Look for the things you haven't seen before. The objects in our daily lives can become as invisible as wallpaper. But when we take the time to really look at something—anything!—we gain insight, understanding, and a more peaceful sense of wonder in the world.

When we focus less on *doing* and more on *being*, expending a little energy on being mindful, our lives improve. Remember: Live in the present. Strive for mindfulness. Every breath is sacred and every moment divine.

8.

A Sense of Humor Can Save Your Life

Life does not cease to be funny when people die any more than it ceases to be serious when people laugh.

—GEORGE BERNARD SHAW

BABCIA KNEW THAT the penalties for stealing were very harsh, and they were rigorously enforced by the communist state. Even taking a small item could get a person sent to the gulag for many years. Babcia herself did not advocate stealing, but she found Stalin's system of enforcement to be very unjust, and especially unfair to the poor who had no means of support.

She had many stories of people who got away with things right under the nose of the oppressive government. She liked to tell and retell these stories, until they became instructional parables or fables of the common man's cleverness. Her favorite story was about a red wheelbarrow.

"There was once a worker," Babcia began, looking at her grandsons. "And this worker lived in the Russian capital. Every day this man worked very hard for very little pay. And every day, when his work was ended, he left the factory to walk home. Every day, he is leaving the building, pushing a red wheelbarrow before him. You see this in your mind?"

The children nodded and smiled, for they had heard this story before; it never failed to delight them.

"Every day, this man is leaving, pushing a shiny red wheelbarrow before him. But Stalin was very worried about stealing. Always, he thought the peasants were trying to steal from him and so he made stealing the worst crime against the state. People who stole were very severely punished."

She sat back and let her words sink in, enjoying the rapt attention on her grandsons' faces. "So. Every day, when this worker left his job, Stalin's guards stopped him at the gate. 'Let us examine your wheelbarrow,' they said. 'We must be sure you are an honest man.' Every day the man stopped at the gate and let the guards inspect his shiny red wheelbarrow. He was very patient. And every day the wheelbarrow was completely empty. Even when they looked underneath they could find nothing that the man was stealing."

Babcia chucked the youngest under the chin. He ducked his head and laughed. "So. Every day the guards inspect and every day they find the worker honest and let him pass. You understand?"

The children nodded, eager for the punchline.

Babcia smiled and rubbed her arms. She leaned toward the boys and tapped a finger against her temple. "But what the guards did not know, is that every day, this worker, he was stealing a brand-new red wheelbarrow."

My FAMILY'S MOST positive reaction to the horrors that we faced was to make light of things whenever possible. Banished to an isolated outpost, considered outsiders, brought there to work for Communism until our bodies gave out, we faced the ultimate in helpless situations. We could easily have given up, as many did. Many were the people who told us, "You were brought here to die." Roughly half of the people sent to Siberia did die, living in fear of an unfeeling system of government enforced by soldiers who themselves felt helpless and who liberally exercised whatever powers they could enforce.

But my grandmother was a fighter. She was angry. Her old life, her dignity, her wealth and property, and even her husband had been stolen from her. And to cap off the indignity of all that loss, she was treated like the lowest form of humanity. The way she dealt with this was to make fun of the government and the soldiers who oppressed her. She could have chosen to react with anger or fear, but instead she chose laughter. She took a look at her enemies and rather than finding them threatening, decided to find them humorous, thereby taking away the threat. It gave her power within her own mind and reframed her thinking until she was less a victim and more a survivor. Humor has the power to change even the most entrenched and painful perceptions.

But you need not be suffering at a Siberian level to use humor to your advantage. In general, we human beings take ourselves much too seriously. In my family, we learned to laugh at ourselves and thereby appreciate each other more. It is a good thing to see the humor in one's own actions. And reaching out to other people, too, becomes so much easier when we do it with humor.

In my clinical practice, I found that if I could make my patients laugh first, they would be more relaxed and more open to new ideas. As Danish-American pianist and humorist Victor Borge said, "A smile is the shortest distance between two people."

When humor enters a relationship, it humanizes it. It creates equality between individuals. It breaks down barriers. Think of the people you feel most comfortable with, the people you love the most. It is very likely that those are the people who make you laugh.

When using humor to bond with another, it is important to remember that what is funny to some may not be to others. Be wary of people who speak in a way that is clearly designed to wound but who then follow their caustic words with, "I'm only kidding." A joke that wounds another person is not a joke. And if you have to justify it, it isn't funny. True humor is embracing and purely fun—it isn't a putdown, and it doesn't mock. True humor makes people feel wonderful. It doesn't separate them or cut them off— instead, it reinforces the understanding that we are all in this together.

To lighten a grim mood, I sometimes tell my patients about a newly discovered disease called Rectal Retinitis. It happens, I tell them, when the nerve from the patient's rectum crosses the nerve from his retina, producing a shitty outlook. They usually nod seriously, then think about it for a moment, then laugh.

When working with groups who are too serious, too stiff and formal (often administrators), I bring in my large collection of funny hats and put a different hat on each person. Within minutes they look around at one another and start giggling and laughing. Now I can work with them. They have become *reachable*.

Scientific research shows that humor has great healing powers. Norman Cousins, who wrote *Anatomy of an Illness as Perceived by the Patient: Reflections on Healing and Regeneration*, initiated the entire field of humor therapy when he claimed he had healed himself with humor and feel-good emotions. Cousins set up a movie projector in his hospital room and watched slapstick movies all day, for many days. He experienced a total cure of his life-threatening illness—a cure the doctors could not explain.

"Always laugh when you can," said Lord Byron. "It is cheap medicine." A sense of humor is one of the most important tools available to us in our human survival kit. If we haven't figured out how to wield our wit by now, we really should take some time and learn to use it.

Back in the early 1970s, before humor therapy was an established method of treatment, I initiated a humor therapy class that became a model for other hospitals in the region; I was frequently asked to give talks about how I had implemented the classes and was encouraged to describe my success rate (which was very high). It was a time when science was just learning what most of us have intuitively understood all our lives: it feels good to laugh, and laughter makes everything just a little bit better.

Laughter has been proven to reduce stress and to promote physical and mental healing, and it also makes helping easier. If we are able to find some small shred of humor in even the most difficult times, we have found a way to ease suffering, to make a connection, and to help others. "A person without a sense of humor," said Henry Ward Beecher, "is like a wagon without springs—jolted by every pebble in the road." I agree. A sense of humor is a shock absorber for the trials of life. We will all hit bumps in the road, but how well we rebound from them largely depends on our ability to see the funny side of any situation. The ability to laugh definitely helped my family survive our Siberian experience.

I have found that counselors and psychotherapists with a good sense of humor are often more effective at treating patients. But "*using* humor" sounds too deliberate, too mechanical. Similarly, any attempt to deconstruct humor generally misses the point. As E. B. White, who wrote the children's classic *Charlotte's Web*, said, "Analyzing humor is like dissecting a frog. Few people are interested and the frog dies of it."

Rather than study and attempt to recreate humor, one has to cultivate, instead, an inner attitude that is based on the belief that there is always a funny side to each situation, no matter how tragic or how serious. You have to believe it. You have to look for it. And if you look for it, you will find it.

There are many types of humor, all of which can be used effectively in helping others. Great orators, ministers, and other public speakers know that the best way to lead in to a speech is to begin with a joke. Make your audience laugh right off, and they will listen better and be more open to your message. Human beings have a tremendous desire, even a *need,* for the release of laughter. Laughter releases tension and promotes bonding.

My family always looked for the humor in any situation we faced. It was common to find humor in things that others might see as terribly unfortunate events. Gallows humor, or black humor, can be a very healing way to examine suffering through a different lens. Here is an example of a silly riddle that employs a bit of gallows humor: "What goes ha, ha, ha, thump?" Answer: "A man laughing his head off." That joke celebrates laughter but also throws in a twist, expanding the joke and taking us in a slightly different direction even as we are laughing. Most successful humor does this.

As the product of a European upbringing, I am very familiar with gallows humor; it has long been a coping mechanism for Europeans during difficult times. Gallows humor makes it easier to handle the major upset of disasters, wars and tragedies. Here is my favorite example of gallows humor:

During the Nazi reign in Germany, when Jews were being pulled from their homes and exterminated, two old Jewish men made an observation: every single day, Hitler walked past their house at eight o'clock in the morning. He was regular as clockwork, every day, eight o'clock in the morning. So the men decided that they would put a large stone on their roof and when Hitler walked past the next morning at eight o'clock, they would drop the heavy rock onto his head—splat—no more Hitler.

The next morning, they sit on the roof, rock at the ready, waiting for Hitler to walk past. Eight o'clock comes, no Hitler. They keep waiting. Nine o'clock comes, still no Hitler. Ten o'clock comes and goes and Hitler never shows up. Finally, one of the men turns to the other and says, "I hope he is all right."

"TATOES?" CRIED A delighted Jurek.

"*Po*tatoes," corrected Andrew, who liked to teach his younger brother things. "You say it, *potatoes*, not tatoes." Teaching Jurek was one of the good things about being an older brother.

Intense concentration played across Jurek's features as his mouth tried to form the new word. "Tatoes," he repeated.

"Yes," said Babcia, touching her younger grandson on the top of his head. "These are from Madame Luchik, from a fortune I told today." She pointed to a pile of brown peelings. "See, Jurek?"

Jurek stepped closer and eyed them hungrily.

"That is a lot," said Andrew, eyes wide.

Babcia's heart swelled with pity to see her grandsons excited by the bounty of a meager pile of peelings. In Poland, every day they'd had more food than they could eat, and a cook to prepare it, too. That her grandsons should now be so grateful for receiving what another person would throw away suddenly pained her. "They are only the peelings," she said.

"Where is the rest of the potato?" Andrew asked.

"It is with Madame Luchik." Babcia felt the pity move aside; a sudden defiance rose up within her. Her grandsons need not be ashamed. They were brave and smart and deserving. "Did you know that Madame Luchik is a foolish woman?" asked Babcia, leaning towards them conspiratorially.

Andrew shook his head, eyes round and innocent.

"She *is* foolish," said Babcia. "She has peeled away the best part of the potato and given it away. She has kept the plain, tasteless, white part for herself, and given us all the vitamins and flavor. We will eat the peelings and be healthier, and it will give us strength to walk all the way to Poland if we have to."

⁓

MY GRANDMOTHER WAS a proud woman. It pained her a great deal to take castoffs to feed her family, but it was even more painful to see her family starving and so she took the castoffs and made the most of them. Her ability to be humble was a wonderful gift she gave us, but it was not the only gift. The gift that lasted so much longer than a dinner of potato peelings was the gift of learning how to see things in the best possible light, often through humor.

Sarcasm is one type of humor, and one that my family frequently employed. When I began to study psychology, I learned that sarcasm is a common human reaction to feelings of helplessness; it is a way to fight back and make the helplessness bearable. Like my grandmother's statement about the potato peelings, sarcasm can be a satisfying replacement for the anger that helplessness generates. In fact, I have come to believe that humor is one of the primary outlets for many human emotions. I have no doubt that sarcasm helped us to survive in Siberia.

People who work in high-stress situations, such as emergency rooms, prisons, counseling centers, and police stations, will tell you how important it is to laugh with your fellow workers. In tense and frustrating situations, humor helps us to relieve stress and function more effectively. "I have seen what a laugh can do," said Bob Hope. "It can transform almost unbearable tears into something bearable, even hopeful." Laughter can improve any situation.

I once worked with a group of patients who were severely mentally disabled. Many had been hospitalized for twenty or thirty years. Each one had a notebook. In his notebook, he wrote down the things that he did in various programs that he attended. It became a running record that served as a way for the patients to get to know themselves, to understand themselves better. Each person in the group had a Polaroid picture of himself pasted onto the front of the notebook. They liked it because they could look at that picture and then talk about themselves as they looked at it. This seemed to be a good approach.

One day a patient in the group said to me, "You know what? We don't know what we look like from behind. We look in the mirror and see ourselves from the front, but we don't ever see the back." This gave me the idea to photograph each one of them from behind and paste that picture on the back of each patient's notebook. In a whimsical way, each patient could then see himself or herself from the front *and* the back, and then inside the book was everything else.

I have always enjoyed the whimsical approach. My dictionary defines whimsical as "full of, or characterized by, whims or whimsy; oddly out of the ordinary, unpredictable." Another definition of whimsy is "a product of playful fancy."

A whimsical approach in dealing with other people is unplanned, spontaneous and intuitive. It creates a playful atmosphere that makes the helper and the receiver of help comfortable and relaxed.

I remember "Richard," a patient in this same group of journal-keepers. For the first few weeks that I knew and worked with Richard, I never saw him laugh or smile. One day, when we were outside, I picked up two rocks and made a sound by hitting them against each other. I told the group that this was the original rock music. That was the first time I saw Richard smile and that was the turning point in his therapy. After that day, he made terrific progress.

Being able to laugh at oneself is extremely important. You will be a more effective helper if you and the person you are helping can see each other as equals. This is best achieved when you don't take yourself too seriously. Make fun of yourself. Be light, rather than heavy.

Humor, laughter, and playfulness lubricate thinking. They are like the oil that makes the machine run better. When you joke and kid around, it creates a relaxed condition, a positive mood. You and the person you are helping become more open, more receptive. Then you can focus on serious matters. You could almost prescribe it.

R: *Before tackling heavy issues, do some heavy laughing first.*

I have found in my years of working with my local hospice, when attending to the needs of the dying individual, that humor plays an important role even there. I remember assisting "Luke," a man very comfortable with the nearness of his own death. Unfortunately, this same air of acceptance could not be attributed to Luke's family. They kept trying desperately to keep him alive. The wife and daughter continually fussed over him, urging him to eat and drink and forcing him to take his medicine until he became quite annoyed with them.

At one point, when I was alone in the room with Luke, I asked him if there was anything I could do to make him more comfortable. His reply? "Yes. Go home…get a gun… come back here…and shoot those women!" We laughed together and I admired his ability to retain a sense of humor to the end.

When I look back now, the irony of that situation becomes clear: Luke's loved ones kept attempting to avoid their feelings of helplessness by fussing over him in a way that left him feeling frustrated and helpless. At the end of his life, weakened and tired of struggling, Luke's sense of humor—shared with me—was the best way he had to fight those helpless feelings and thereby empower himself for the difficult days ahead of him.

9.

Empowering Others Is the Best Way to Help Them

Ultimately the only power to which man should aspire is
that which he exercises over himself.

—ELIE WIESEL

"HERE, ANDREW." BABCIA handed her grandson a large, flat-capped black mushroom, from a cache of them held in her apron.

The child took the mushroom in his hands and turned it over. He smelled the underside. "Where did you find them this time?"

"In the same place, Andrew. But, shh, do not tell, or the whole village will be picking from our secret mushroom patch." She placed her hand on her grandson's head and smiled. "You can put it on the grate now."

A small fire burned in a pot with a makeshift grate over the top; the child laid the mushroom—cap-down—onto the grate.

"Good. Just like that," she said. "That will keep the juices inside."

Andrew loved the large, wild, black mushrooms. His grandmother had shown him the spot where they emerged each fall, and taught him the best time to harvest them—when the caps had opened fully, like an umbrella, but the edges were still firm. It was his task to cook them, and he felt very adult tending the fire, carefully moving the mushrooms until they were tender and juicy. His mouth watered at the thought of biting into one. Tender, juicy, and smoky, they were like soft meat cooked over a fire. For days they'd had no food other than a few pieces of pasty flatbread made from flour and salt.

"I will send Jurek out with the metal bowl to put them in."

"Yes, Grandmother," said Andrew, pursing his mouth as he carefully added another mushroom to the grate. It was not said out loud, but the child knew how important this job was. He was six years old, and he was helping to feed his family.

I CAN STILL remember the delicious aroma of those mushrooms cooking and the pride I felt when roasting them. Not only did they taste wonderful and fill the belly with warmth, they were work that *I* had done to feed the family, something I could be proud of. Cooking mushrooms gave me a deep sense of accomplishment and worth, and helped me to understand the importance of my role in keeping my family from starving. To this day, I love cooking for my loved ones and watching them eat.

I believe my grandmother (a wise woman) knew exactly what she was doing when she let me cook those mushrooms—she was empowering me, though she would not have used that language. She knew how important it was to keep us all involved, to keep us invested in our joint survival.

We all need to have a purpose. Human beings thrive when the purpose is clear and we are able to achieve it. Often, those who are unhappy simply have not found a purpose, have not learned how to work to reach their goals, or have not taken the time to help others reach theirs. Viktor Frankl said, "Ever more people today have the means to live, but no meaning to live for."

Paying attention to the needs of others is very important. I mean really paying attention—even when it goes against your own desires. Remember the fellow I met through my local hospice, who wanted me to shoot his caregivers? Those caregivers were listening more to their own desire to keep him alive than to his personal need to be done living. Sadly, they let their own fears and anxieties get in the way of what was best for their loved one.

When I look back on my life, I realize that my purpose has been to help and empower others, and much of that help consisted of teaching. Teaching people how to deal with their problems, teaching them new life skills, teaching them different ways to look at life, or helping them to understand the purpose of their own lives gave them confidence. It gave them their very own stash of personal power. This all boils down to one of my most central beliefs, that empowering others is the very best way to help them. This idea of empowerment has been expressed many different ways. My favorite is the maxim "*Give* a man a fish, feed him for a day. *Teach* a man to fish, feed him for life."

In my experience, the best psychotherapists and counselors do not solve people's problems for them. They teach people how to solve their own problems. They empower them. Think back to the four results of giving advice and you will recall that trying to solve another person's problems rarely works. Instead they are left feeling either dependent (if it works) or resentful (if it doesn't).

In fact, if I don't believe I can help a client within eight sessions, I won't take them on. I don't believe in long-term therapy. If I can't help you in eight weeks, then I'm not the therapist for you. As mentioned before, I expect my clients to do homework, which often surprises them. But teaching is a form of sharing, and sharing has always been important to me, probably a result of my early training in survival. By the age of six, I knew very solidly that sharing knowledge and resources helps keep everyone alive. When we have something of value, it is not enough to enjoy it ourselves, we must share it.

When we share, we increase not only the value of the shared object but our enjoyment of it. Imagine the flame of a candle. I can light a thousand candles from that one candle, and the light of the initial candle is not diminished in any way, but so much more light has been spread around.

Helping others, sharing the light of our candle, helps us all. Here is a translation of a Hindu proverb: "Help your brother's boat across, and your own will reach the shore." This is a perfect expression of the global value of helping.

All of my life I've had a great thirst for knowledge. And I've also had a strong desire to share what I've learned with others. I've come to discover that in order to truly master a topic, I need to teach it to someone else. This is true of most people—we only fully grasp a concept once we've passed it on. Showing the other person that you can learn from them also empowers them to see themselves in a new and stronger light.

Everyone we meet is our teacher. This is especially true of those we interact with on a regular basis: our spouses, children, coworkers, friends, patients, students, etc. Everyone teaches us something, even if it is something as simple as how lucky we are—or how selfish. Because we are all connected, each of us has some skill, idea, or wisdom that can be shared with others in a way that will help them. We all have the ability to empower one another. Can you imagine a world where everyone did just that? If we all worked together to empower one another, we could end disease, solve world hunger, save the planet, and be home in time for dinner.

Instead, we too often wring our hands and shake our heads. *Whatever can we do?*

Powerlessness is the disease of our times. Feelings of powerlessness are usually at the core of anyone's unhappiness. And the modern tendency to blame others for our problems doesn't help matters any—in fact, it contributes to our sense of powerlessness. It may be popular to blame our parents, society, government, bosses, or even spouses for our troubles, but one of the best ways to empower people is to help them understand their own free will and teach them how to exercise that free will in the choices they make every day.

We can empower ourselves by accepting that we have responsibility for our own lives, or we can wring our hands in frustration and helplessness. We have the choice. In successful psychotherapy the client gradually learns to accept responsibility for his life. And the good news is that you don't need an advanced degree in psychology to help others become empowered. It's empowering simply to learn, to realize, to believe, and to exercise free will.

To my patients I say, "Repeat after me: *I am not the slave of my past but the master of my future. Whatever situation I am in is a result of decisions and choices I have made. I am continuously creating my reality with my thoughts and my decisions. Everything I do, think, feel and decide now is creating the reality in which I will live in the future.*" This kind of verbalization can be very powerful.

It is also of prime importance that we learn to *accept responsibility for our feelings*. What does that mean? It means that instead of saying, "*You made* me angry," we learn to say, "*I am* angry." It is healthier and more empowering to own up to our feelings, even our negative ones—perhaps most especially our negative ones. Listen to the difference in the following statements and imagine you are saying them to someone you love: "You have really disappointed me" versus "I am very disappointed by your actions." When in doubt, always try to begin a statement of feelings with "I" and you will learn to speak for yourself and not blame others.

When we learn to accept that our thoughts, our interpretation of events, and the stories we tell ourselves make us unhappy, we can learn to tell ourselves new stories, think positive thoughts, reinterpret past events and thereby become happier.

Here's an example: Instead of accepting that it is raining, that the earth needs rain, that it nourishes everything on the planet, we often choose to create a story that makes us feel bad instead: *What an awful, dreary day.* Negative thinking and depression go hand in hand. As Carl Jung said, "If you are depressed, you are too high up in your mind."

Overcoming fear is also empowering. There is an interesting phenomenon that most psychotherapists accept—the more you talk about your fear, the weaker it gets. The more you avoid the fear, the stronger it gets. Therefore, encouraging our loved ones to talk about their fears is actually helping them to become empowered.

After listening to a loved one's fears, many people want to help them fix those fears. But as we have firmly established by now (I hope!), advice and solutions can be tricky fields to navigate—more like minefields for the inexperienced. But never fear, I have a solution for you—and it is an absurdly simple one. When a loved one comes to you with a problem, seeking advice, the very best response of all is to listen attentively, mirror her emotions for her, and then offer your firm confidence, your belief in her ability to solve the problem herself. With conviction, you can offer some version of, "I believe you'll make the right decision," or "I'm confident you'll figure out the best solution." It is empowering just to know that others believe in us, that people stand behind us, and chances are good that your confidence will give your friend enough of her own confidence to make the decision that she probably knew all along was the right one.

Even our diets can help us to feel empowered. We know what food is good for us and what food we should avoid, and yet most of us ignore that knowledge. One good example is sugar. Eating too much sugar can lead to obesity and diabetes, yet most of us eat a lot of sugar, which in effect means that we are, as Lois Levy (*Undress Your Stress*) says, "sugaring ourselves to death."

The same can be said of fat, too many calories, and too much caffeine, all of which can negatively affect our thinking, mood, and feelings. When I am able to convince my patients to improve their diet, they feel better and gain a sense of control over their existence. And, as the ancient philosopher Seneca wrote, "Most powerful is he who has himself in his own power."

⁓

YOUNG ANDREW CARRIED an empty bowl as he crossed the open field then carefully stepped rock-to-rock across a wide stream. The breeze blew his hair around and moved softly against his skin. A field of yellow wildflowers spread before him; birds twittered in the bushes and splashed at the edges of the stream. For all its dreadful, draining winters, Siberia in summer felt like a blessing, a wonder. The days were as long and full of sunshine as the winter ones were endless and cold. And Andrew had a very important mission on this day—a secret place to visit. Why he had never seen anyone else cross the stream and enter the field, he couldn't say, but this magical meadow felt like his and his alone.

As the sound of the stream faded behind him, he could already see the bright red shapes peeking out from the leaves on the ground before him. Careful not to squash them, he knelt, the bright summer sun beating down on the back of his neck, and began to fill the metal bowl with berries. *Plink, plink, plunk*, slowly the small, wild strawberries covered the bottom. The softest of them left his fingers shining with red juice and filled his head with the heady scent of summer. His stomach growled and he longed to eat a giant fistful of berries, but he thought of his mother and grandmother at home, and of his little brother Jurek.

Earlier in the year, Jurek had been sent to the Communist preschool to begin his education. Although Andrew had fought successfully against attending the school, Jurek was younger and had not escaped conscription. He had even been excited to attend. Babcia and Zosia believed in education, even if the Communist school was an attempt to espouse the rightness of Stalin's vision for his people, starting with the children. But the adults knew that Jurek would be fed a meager lunch at the school and with their resources stretched so pitifully thin, any meal for any member of the family meant more food for all.

What they had not expected of the young boy was that he would secretly bring home a portion of his food to share with his family. Each day, three-year-old Jurek pocketed a slice of bread—even though it was against the rules—and brought it home, despite his own overwhelming hunger. Andrew had seen and benefited from this act of selfless generosity and he was determined to make his own meaningful contribution to the family food supply.

His stomach growled again as an especially ripe berry squished between his fingers. "Just one," he told himself, "a squished one." He placed the shapeless berry in his mouth and sucked on his sweetened fingers. While he continued to fill the small bowl, he held the one soft, sweet strawberry in his mouth, letting it melt onto his tongue as he daydreamed of the surprise and pleasure he would see on his mother's face when he held out a bowl filled with sweet red strawberries.

TO THIS DAY, I remember spending many hours gathering those wild strawberries by the stream. At the end of the day

I felt so proud presenting a bowl of berries to my family. Early in my life, I learned that every contribution, no matter how small, is important. I learned to value whatever I could do to make a bad situation even slightly better. This is an important lesson that we all need to remember, especially when we are feeling powerless. Small actions can and do make a difference. A small rock thrown into a lake can create ripples that eventually reach the shore.

Even my little brother, the youngest of us all, taught us a lesson in sharing and survival. He had not intended to teach anything, of course, but simply wanted to share his good fortune with those he loved who were not so fortunate. The memory of his innocent selflessness inspires me to this day. He was a thoughtful boy who grew into a thoughtful man.

Tragically, my talented younger brother was killed in the prime of his life. He was hit by a car while riding his bicycle, training for a biathlon, leaving me the sole remaining survivor from our time in Siberia. At the time of his death, Jurek was a devoted husband and father. He was also a well-loved and prominent professor of astrophysics at Princeton University. When news of his death reached the university, classes were shut down for the day. Jurek's design contributions produced some of the first space vehicles ever launched, and he called himself friend to a number of America's famous first astronauts. My brother's selfless nature, his kindness, and his ability to empower others professionally and personally lives on in the many lives he touched.

"We are formed and molded by our thoughts," said Buddha. "Those whose minds are shaped by selfless thoughts give joy when they speak or act. Joy follows them like a shadow that never leaves them." That description fits my brother Jurek.

Another way to become empowered is to fully realize the way in which negative thoughts cause feelings of weakness and powerlessness. If we say things such as, "I am a loser" or "I am weak," then we come to believe them and behave accordingly. With our words and thoughts, we create our own reality. We make real what we speak and think. This is a sobering thought in itself. Happily, we have the power to change our thoughts—and it requires nothing more than a conscious change in attitude, a deliberate modification of perspective.

Words, once spoken and shared, have even more power than thoughts. The vibration of the voice, when added to the originating thought, makes the thought more powerful and focuses it more directly into the physical world.

When my patients do homework between sessions, they become active participants in their therapy so that I can honestly say, "You did as much as I did—pat yourself on the back" and it makes their treatment progress much more rapidly than it otherwise would.

I once had a patient I'll call Meg, who was convinced she was unattractive. She had no deformity or unusual physical circumstances, and plenty of people in her life told her she was attractive, but she had become so convinced of her ugliness that she had trouble looking in the mirror. If she did look in a mirror, all she saw was her perceived cosmetic failings. She believed it, so she saw it—a sort of anorexia of beauty. In therapy Meg and I worked on her larger issues of personal self-esteem, but for her homework, I kept it simple. She was to spend time each day looking into the mirror and speaking to her reflection. What she was instructed to say was also simple: "I am attractive. I have a unique and precious life force that springs from within. I am attractive." By the end of our therapy sessions, Meg's self-confidence in her appearance had increased to the point where she carried herself with more pride and smiled more often. And lo and behold! Even though her basic physical appearance had not changed, her improved posture and her confident smile actually made her more beautiful.

"Gene," another patient of mine, was convinced that he couldn't compete on an intellectual level. "I'm so stupid," he often said, convincing himself anew each time he uttered the words. To Gene, I gave a card with a printed statement that read, "I am intelligent." His homework was to stand in front of a mirror and repeat the sentence one hundred times each day. Within two weeks, his thoughts and feelings about himself began to change.

Despite extensive evidence to the contrary, most people still do not believe that they can choose what they think at any given moment. It can be an earthshaking discovery to suddenly understand that you do have the power—the power to choose what you think and therefore what you project.

Think about it. If you dwell on a positive memory, or anticipate some positive experience, you will notice that you become more relaxed and feel better. Remembering happy memories or imagining happy outcomes lowers the blood pressure and helps relieve stress. Many people also believe that it brings more good things into your life.

Worrying is the opposite. It's basically imagining bad things happening in the future. Looking at the future negatively will result in unnecessary tension, anxiety, stress, and general bad feelings. It can also affect your health. Winston Churchill said, "You create your own universe as you go along." How succinct, and how true.

I often teach that the opposite of worry is to visualize good things happening in the future. Imagine the following scenario: two people are going for an important job interview. One of them worries about all the things that could go wrong. He could trip when entering the room, he could stutter or say something stupid, he could spill something on his tie beforehand. As a result, he spends a lot of energy visualizing the very things he doesn't want to happen. His fear and anxiety grow exponentially.

The other interviewee spends his hour visualizing the interview in a positive manner. He pictures himself sitting relaxed, saying all the right things, handling it well. He even visualizes the interviewer's pleased response—that what he says is well received. Which of the two interview candidates do you think will have a better interview? There have been many studies that show that the second man does much better.

Some attribute this to a phenomenon called the Law of Attraction. Very simply put, it states that whatever you spend your time imagining is what you bring forth in your life. The energy that you give to a thought (either positive or negative) attracts more of the same. Like attracts like. Therefore, positive thoughts bring about positive changes. This certainly proved true during my family's ordeal in Siberia.

The flip side is that negative thoughts bring about negative changes, so we are much better off when we limit the negative thoughts that we all too often let consume us. Don't spend your time thinking about all the things you haven't accomplished. Don't dwell on the mistakes you've made in the past. Don't spend your time dreading the future. Such thinking increases your negative energy and, in turn, the likelihood of a negative reality. It also makes you feel unhappy and hopeless in the process.

Instead, imagine a new life unfolding before you, a life filled with possibilities. Spend time daydreaming of a hopeful future or a positive outcome and you take the first step toward improving every aspect of your life. Simply put, one of the best ways to turn your dreams into reality is to have faith.

10.

Have Faith

We are not human beings having a spiritual experience.
We are spiritual beings having *a human experience.*

—PIERRE TEILHARD DE CHARDIN

IT WAS LATE August and the harvest moon had been wan-
ing for a week. The potatoes had already been removed
from the field nearest Babcia's hut. The villagers assigned to
work there had moved on to other tasks. The potatoes now
sat in the village storehouse, waiting to be carried off by
train and dispensed to the Communist state. Whatever had
escaped the harvesters or been rejected by them now lay in
the fields to molder. Babcia could almost feel the fat spuds
sitting on top of the ground, waiting. But it was against the
law to return to the fields and glean.

Of all the laws that the Communists imposed on them
in Siberia, Babcia felt that this one was perhaps the most

abominable. Perfectly good vegetables left to rot in the fields or on the vines while people—mostly women and children—starved in their homes. Yes, she knew the rationale: if it were not illegal to glean leftover produce, then workers might deliberately leave the best vegetables in the field and return later to retrieve them. And yet, the attempt at curtailing such behavior hurt the innocent and robbed them of perfectly good food—food that would rot in the sun. This was food for the taking that was illegal to take. The injustice of it made Babcia want to spit nails.

Instead, she waited until the moon was not so bright, wore her darkest clothes, and sneaked back into the fields in the early hours of the morning. She risked her life to do this, but for the sake of her starving grandchildren, she would take that risk. Besides, the vegetables were going to rot! How did that make sense? It did not, and no amount of explaining could make it so.

But breaking the law was not something Babcia liked to do. She was a law-abiding citizen. She did not wish any trouble on her family. In the four nights since the harvest she had struggled mightily within herself, mentally weighing her options.

In the end, Babcia's practical side won out over her law-abiding side. There was food available. It was nearby, and it was free. She could not continue to count her grandsons' ribs and do nothing. She would risk her own capture and imprisonment.

Babcia took a moment to pray before going out to glean in the nearby field. "Heavenly Father," she began, "please forgive what I am about to do this night in the name of my starving grandchildren. Please guide my hand that I might do thy will out in the fields and not follow my own selfish needs. If it is your will, please help me to save my grandchildren from starvation. They have wasted away so that I hardly recognize them."

FOR ALL OF her life, my grandmother was a devout Catholic. She tried hard to be a good person and a good citizen, too. She did not believe in stealing, but neither did she believe that it was right to allow good food to rot in the fields while her family starved. In fact, *not* giving her grandchildren food that would ultimately go to waste felt more like stealing—stealing food from innocent children. And so, when she knew there were leftover vegetables in the fields, she sneaked out, gathered them up, and brought them home to us. If caught, my grandmother could have been shot, and yet she was determined to keep her family from starving no matter the risk.

Even as she struggled to keep us alive, my grandmother

worried terribly about whether her actions would be considered sins by the Catholic Church. She suffered a great deal of guilt for breaking the law—any law—even one that so senselessly discriminated against women, children, and the poor. Upon leaving Siberia, the first thing my grandmother asked to do was visit a church and speak to a priest. After taking her lengthy confession, the priest assured her that the things she had done in Siberia to keep her family alive were not sins. When she left the church that day, a tremendous burden had been lifted from her heart.

In Siberia, I learned that the spiritual surrounds us. It is available at all times to anyone who chooses to look for it. And for the majority of people, access to their spiritual side is an important aspect of mental health and wellbeing. Unfortunately, it is also a frequently neglected side. We go to the gym, we eat right, take our vitamins, dress warmly if the weather is cold… and yet, too often, we forget to exercise our spiritual side, feed our souls with spiritual teachings, take our daily prayer vitamin, and wrap ourselves in the warmth of the spirit.

We've established that hope is important, and that striving to make our hope a reality is necessary, but an element of faith is an equally necessary component of our lives. Indira Gandhi stated this idea succinctly when she said, "The purpose of life is to believe, to hope, and to strive."

Yet many professionals avoid the discussion of spiritual

issues. If a patient brings up spiritual concerns, most therapists refer the patient to a clergyman or priest. "Love" and "God" are words not often heard in clinical therapy, but in my work as a psychotherapist I cannot imagine excluding spirituality as an issue or topic. Spirituality is an important, even *essential,* part of life for most people, and, as such, I am comfortable discussing it.

That does not mean, however, that I espouse a specific religion or approach. I understand spirituality as *the recognition that there is something beyond our physical existence, that there exists a reality which we cannot see or measure with our scientific instruments, and that each one of us is more than just a highly developed mammal.* The "something beyond" is our soul or spirit and is related to God and life after death. All religious and spiritual paths begin here, and how my patients choose to access their own spirituality is their personal choice.

Gary Zukav, in his book *The Seat of the Soul*, describes a spiritual approach in psychology as "a disciplined and systematic study of what is necessary to the health of the soul." He suggests that we need to identify those behaviors and attitudes that are harmful to the soul, such as brutality, dishonesty, irrationality, and nonforgiveness. Once identified, we can eliminate them, for such negative attitudes are poisons to the spiritual soul.

In working with patients, I try to differentiate between an approach that begins in the mind and an approach that begins in the heart. Working from the head is based on book learning—what I learned in graduate school and from publications I have read on the topic of psychology and treatment—and it has been valuable, to be sure. But now, after more than forty years in practice, I have learned the value of working mostly from the heart. Working from the heart feels more genuine, more authentic. It has definitely been more spiritual. Recently I learned that the word "psychology" in Chinese translates as "science of the heart," and that seems right to me.

I look at helping others as a spiritual experience, as a type of service, based on the idea that each one of us is "our brother's keeper." I am convinced that all of our difficulties—at the root level—deal with spiritual issues and that the most effective way of helping others is always to be aware of this.

John Diamond, MD, author of *Life Energy: Unlocking the Hidden Power of Your Emotions to Achieve Total Well-Being*, says, "The course through life is determined by hundreds of thousands—by millions—of choices. What to feel, what to want, what to say, what to eat, what to do. And each and every choice is for health, for love and for God—or not. Thus all are spiritual decisions."

"Ralph" was someone most of my colleagues did not want as a patient. Ralph was angry with God. He felt that he had done everything that was required of him by his religion. He was a good man, and yet terrible things were happening to him. He was angry. How could God do this to him? In the course of his treatment, we had long discussions about his understanding of God's role in his life, about how he perceived God and his relationship to him. As a result of these discussions, and some assigned reading, Ralph eventually stopped being angry with God and with his situation, and he was able to resume his normal, loving attitude toward life.

A spiritual approach to dealing with others means recognizing your fellow human as a spiritual being, as a soul. To patients who are receptive to spiritual concepts, I will explain that we need to work together in psychotherapy, work to recognize that each individual is made up of three equally important parts. The first is the physical body, with its own needs for nutrition, exercise, sleep, maintenance, care. The second is the human being whose thoughts and feelings are very important to functioning as a healthy person—most mental health professionals place the bulk of their attention on this second part. The third is the spiritual side of our being; the needs of that being are equally important. Thus, in my work with patients, I address their spiritual needs in addition to their physical and emotional needs.

THE FAMILY GATHERED close in the hut. Babcia encouraged them—with a wave of her hand—to come together. Even though the Communist state forbade religious observance of any kind, Babcia refused to follow that law. In her mind, there was a higher law at work: God's law. And she would not neglect God's law. She had felt the presence of God protecting them throughout their ordeal in Siberia—she would not disrespect that. Babcia believed in miracles, and the fact that they were even still alive felt like a miracle on most days. It was time to spend a few minutes being thankful.

Babcia lowered herself to the floor and the children sat down beside her. "Come, Zosia," she called, and her daughter moved nearer and joined them on the floor. She was not ashamed to be humble.

Together, the family's first offering of thankfulness would be to recite the Lord's Prayer. "Our Father," they began, "who art in heaven, hallowed be thy name." The themes in that prayer, of giving one's own will over to God's, of asking for forgiveness, help in avoiding temptation, and deliverance from evil spoke to Babcia's hope and belief in the rightness of the world. She wanted this faith she shared with her family to heal and lift up her grandsons as well as it had lifted her for more than fifty years. She saw prayer as a necessary aspect of her faith, but also as a gift she could pass along to them.

The children knew the words by now and spoke them with their mother and grandmother, and their communal voices, lifted in the same prayer, flowed through their bodies. The combined voices gave the prayer a power all its own—a power to make good things happen, to make the prayers become real. Daily prayer was a balm for their battered lives.

And then, when the Lord's Prayer was finished, Babcia would speak her own prayer aloud for the benefit of the family. "Dear Heavenly Father, thank you for this day and for the many blessings you have given to us. Thank you for my beautiful daughter and my two fine, strong young grandsons. Please hold them in your mercy and keep them safe. And remember their father Vincent, wherever he may be. If it is your will, please guide Vincent's path that he may find us in this desolate place and carry us home. We ask this in the name of the Father and of the Son and of the Holy Spirit. Amen."

Always Babcia remembered to ask that her family be delivered of their suffering, be delivered from Siberia, so long as it was God's will.

CATHOLICISM WAS MY grandmother's religion; the patterns of prayer and the daily rituals fed her soul. As I grew older, I found a different spiritual path from my grandmother's, but I am still grateful for her early teachings. As a child, I learned a great deal about the needs of the soul from her. She never neglected that aspect of her life or our lives.

As an adult, I have learned even more about the soul from Gary Zukav, a spiritual adviser and motivational speaker who leads what he calls Omega Weekends, one of which I was fortunate enough to attend in July 2000. During that weekend, Gary confirmed many of the beliefs that I had already begun to understand intuitively. He explained that the needs of the soul are usually opposite to those of the ego. The ego, he said, wants us to compete in everything. The soul wants us to cooperate in all endeavors. The ego wants more of everything for itself; the soul wants to share with others. The ego thrives on conflict; the soul thrives on harmony and reverence for life. The ego loves action; the soul loves stillness, silence, and beauty.

Goethe said, "A man should hear a little music, read a little poetry, and see a fine picture every day of his life, in order that worldly cares may not obliterate the sense of the beautiful, which God has implanted in the human soul."

If you look at your fellow humans from the point of view of their souls, you will see that helping others is a response to the needs of the soul—both theirs and yours. And responding to the needs of the soul is always a good thing. Mother Teresa said, "Let no one ever come to you without leaving better and happier." Individuals who are committed to a life of service—like Mother Teresa—are putting aside the needs of their ego and responding to the needs of their soul.

My guess is that in our daily lives, we devote most of our time, effort, and energy to the needs of the ego and only a small percentage of our time to the needs of the soul. I believe that we would all benefit greatly if we increased our focus on the needs of our souls. Introspection or meditation allows us to get in touch with these soul needs. From that perspective, "helping" becomes a natural flow, effortless, straight from the heart.

Prayer and visualizations can also be used to help people, even from a great distance. Research has shown that prayers and good thoughts can help those who are recovering from an illness to recover more quickly. And I have personally experienced the dramatic results of positive visualizations. Here's what I mean by positive visualizations: You can imagine, very vividly, something desirable happening, either to you, or to someone else. You can focus your energy and the energy of others onto this one thought, this one image of how you would like things to be. And that energy can generate a transformative and mysterious power that makes the visualization become reality.

As an example, I knew of a meditation group that was trying to help one of its members. She was not able to attend the meeting because she was sick at home, so the group visualized (imagined) her surrounded by roses, which they believed would have a healing effect. The next day, she reported that the previous evening she had smelled roses all over her house. She did not know of the group's efforts on her behalf, and she did feel better.

"Clarice" was an individual that my meditation group wanted to help. She lay in the hospital, suffering after a serious accident that had caused significant liver damage. Clarice was unconscious and her prognosis was poor. Our group came together and in the course of our meeting visualized her liver surrounded by ice cubes (to lower the fever) and lemons (to bring down the swelling). She did not know of our efforts. We found out later that on that same evening, she woke up and her first words were, "May I have some lemonade?" Clarice made a full recovery and later returned to the group to thank us in person.

I often tell my clients and students that visualizations are the opposite of worrying. Worrying is being powerless and sitting alone—high up in your mind—imagining a negative outcome. Visualization is imagining a positive outcome and doing whatever is within your power to make it a reality. When trying to help someone in a general way, visualize them happy, relaxed, and at peace. There is a great deal of evidence that this works.

When you look at life from a spiritual perspective, you become aware of the miraculous nature of the events in your life. Often things that might have been seen as coincidence or luck take on a new luster. My survival in Siberia could certainly be considered miraculous. I believe that life is full of miracles—we just choose not to see them. As Albert Einstein said, "There are only two ways to live your life. One is as though nothing is a miracle. The other is as though everything is a miracle."

11.

Choose the Right Source of Motivation

A person who does not have anything to believe in is
without energy.

—THICH NHAT HANH

FENDRICK RETURNED TO the small hut where Babcia and
Zosia lived with the children. After the night that Babcia
prayed for him, he had knocked every time he returned to
their hut. No longer did he just walk in.

As usual, he had been drinking, but he was merely jolly as
he handed over a few biscuits he had saved from his rations. "It
is not much," he said with a smile as Zosia took them from his
hand, "but I could give you more—if you would marry me."

Zosia was used to his proposals by now. Many Polish
women who came to the village without their husbands
ended up marrying Russian soldiers who were assigned to
their camp. They were alone, afraid, they were watching

their children slowly starve to death, and everyone in the village assured them that there would be no leaving Siberia. Some told themselves it was merely for survival. Some had benefits withheld until they agreed. Some did it for their children.

But Zosia always planned to reunite with her husband. She could not imagine taking Fendrick as a new husband when she was certain her real husband was alive and would come looking for them someday.

"If I were to marry you, what would I tell my husband when he came to find me?" she asked Fendrick in a voice that was clever but firm.

"You will tell him you are Russian now. I will tell him you are Russian."

"He would be very unhappy if I said that. I think I'd better not marry you today," she replied, moving him gently toward the door as she spoke. "But thank you for the biscuits, Fendrick. The children thank you."

"Thank you," cried the children from across the room.

"God bless you, Fendrick," said Babcia with a sly smile, their now standard joke.

The next day in the barn, Zosia told Marya about Fendrick asking her again to marry him.

"Why do you continue to say no?" asked Marya. "Don't you want protection?"

"Such protection costs too much. I have a husband."

"Yes, but where is this husband while you are starving?"

"We have food."

"I have seen your little Andrew. He walks on sticks. He is all elbows, that one."

The truth in those words made Zosia's throat hurt. Tears stung the back of her eyes. Watching her young sons daily waste away was more painful than she could express. But she believed that her husband would find them. And they could hold out a little longer, just a few more days, she told herself. One day at a time she waited, and just when she would consider giving up, another gift of food would come. Zosia would not let her children starve, but neither would she throw away their old lives by marrying a Russian soldier. She shook her head and looked toward the open door of the barn.

"My husband will come for us," she said.

MY MOTHER WAS a beautiful woman. She had many opportunities to use her beauty to change her circumstances, but her primary motivation was to leave Siberia and keep her children alive until that could happen. She approached our survival with a single-mindedness that gave us all hope and belief in its eventual reality. I'm guessing that the repeated offers of regular food and better shelter were tempting, if not for her, then as a way to save us, her children. But my mother stood steadfast and gently refused each soldier who offered to marry her and keep her safe. She kept her eyes on the future, on my father's return. She loved him. She did not want to marry a Russian soldier. She did not want to live in Russia forever.

What motivates us to take action in our lives? Usually, we *do* know what needs to be done, what we *want* to do, what is the right thing to do, and what we should do. The energy to pursue what we want to do or should do is called motivation. All too often, we find ourselves lacking in motivation or lacking in the right kind of motivation.

To *motivate* is to provide a motive that prompts a person to act in a certain way; it determines volition and moves one to action. I've come to believe that the energy we call motivation is primarily generated by our beliefs. Thich Nhat Hanh, a Zen Buddhist Vietnamese monk, has said, "When you have faith, you have a lot of energy." Faith also gives you patience and the ability to take the long view in terms of motivation. Often, choosing the right source of motivation is the difference between choosing what is easy and at hand, although not ideal, and having the trust, faith, and perseverance to pursue what is more difficult but which we know to be the right course of action. Like my mother in

Siberia—even starving and seeing her children starving, she waited for my father to return. Her choice was often painful and difficult, but it was the right choice and it eventually paid off for all of us.

I believe it is important that we examine our motives and take the time to ask ourselves, "Why am I doing this?" Unfortunately, this kind of deep introspection most often occurs only in psychotherapy. If only we could all learn to look inside ourselves on a daily basis, to access our inner feelings and motivations, then perhaps the therapists of the world would all be out of work—and what a triumph that would be. (Yes, even if it left me unemployed!)

Examining our motivation is the first step in understanding our actions. If I believe that my personal survival is more important than any other principle, my motivation will be greatly influenced by that. If, however, I believe that there are other values or principles that are equally important, I could be motivated in a different direction. My grandfather, for instance, was motivated by a concept beyond that of his own survival when he starved to death so the rest of us could have a chance to live.

Understanding your motives is like looking in a mirror. And if you look with your eyes wide open, you may not like what you see.

The beliefs that govern human behavior are generated

from two sources: our soul and our ego. And we need to pay attention to both of them, even though their needs usually oppose each other.

The ego is concerned with our survival—our popularity, being right, competing successfully, winning, and having more of everything. Our souls, by contrast, motivate us in the direction of sharing, cooperation, gratitude, unconditional love, and living in the present. I believe that most of our motivation is a blend of the two but that too often we get the blend in the wrong percentages—mostly ego, not enough soul. Henry David Thoreau expressed the importance of nurturing both parts of the human experience when he wrote, "Good for the body is the work of the body and good for the soul is the work of the soul and good for either is the work of the other."

In Siberia, the motives of ego and soul blended well in my family. Even though survival was the main issue, it was not the survival of the individual but always the survival of the unit, the whole family. We all took care of each other. Each one of us contributed to our collective survival.

During the summer, we would gather dried cow dung in the field. If we didn't have enough by the end of the summer we would freeze to death during the winter. This was the main fuel in the cold season, which lasted many months. When we help each other as a family, as a nation, as a group of fellow human beings, we are responding to a source of motivation that helps ourselves but that also helps the collective whole. This principle of helping each other has always been a strong force of motivation in my life.

In my work with clients, it always seemed desirable and beneficial to pay more attention to the needs of the soul, since the soul is most often neglected in our modern culture. Modern culture tends toward materialism, focuses primarily on the ego, and often ignores the needs of the soul. But this is not a wise approach to living, for when the motivations of the soul are not attended to, frustration and anger often fester and build, and when that happens, it is the whole human that suffers.

BABCIA BLAMED THE Russian army in general and Stalin in particular for her family's wretched predicament. She knew they would not be facing such hardships if not for Stalin's orders to banish wealthy, educated Poles from their homeland to pave the way for communism. She was angry, but one did not complain about the government. Complaints against the communist leader were punishable by death. So Babcia did not complain, but still, she had many things to say.

"The Russian soldiers," she told her daughter, "are very clever men. They spend a great deal of time acquiring time."

Zosia wrinkled her eyebrows and gave her mother a puzzled look.

Babcia pulled up her sleeve; she tapped her bare wrist.

Then her daughter smiled with understanding. "Yes," she agreed. "And very stylish, too. Most Polish men, if they have a watch, have only the one."

"Not the Russian men," said Babcia. "Russian men love the wristwatch. One dapper fellow in the village yesterday had six watches on one arm."

"All bought and paid for, of course," said Zosia, with a sly glance at her mother.

"No doubt," replied Babcia. "And all coordinated so well with his uniform."

"Very fancy," her daughter agreed. "But I wonder. Does this mean that the Russian soldiers have too much time on their hands?"

"Or on their wrists?" asked Babcia, suppressing a chuckle; the children laughed to see the grown-ups being mischievous.

"They are cultured, too," said Zosia when she had composed herself.

"Certainly," chuckled Babcia, wiping at her eyes. "I will remember until the day I die how they pounded on our door when they first invaded Poland, demanding to know where the delousing stations were."

"They couldn't find them."

"No, they could not. And one soldier said, 'This is because Poland is a very uncivilized country. Any country without a place to remove lice from a man is not a modern country.' I remember they were very upset."

"Yes, very upset. And you told them why we had no delousing stations?"

"I told him, 'It is true we have no such stations in our country. I do not know what is this *louse* you speak of. My whole life, I have never seen one. I have never seen a louse.' When he turned to leave the house, I could not help but mutter, '…until now.'"

EVEN NORMALLY DESTRUCTIVE emotions like frustration and anger can be turned around and used as a source of motivation for positive change. There are many examples of this in the world and there are many examples from my family's time in Siberia. My grandmother took her anger at the Russian government and first turned it into humor, then turned it into a motivating force behind her desire to survive and leave Siberia. Leaving would be her ultimate revenge against the brutal, unfeeling system that had cast her family aside, caused her husband to starve himself to death, and forced them all to live in conditions of privation and near starvation.

The Roman Stoic philosopher Epictetus wrote, "First say to yourself what you would be; and then do what you have to do." This is a perfect expression of how we must first examine our desires in order to find our motivation, and then pursue the goal, always with an eye toward our initial motivation.

As in my mother's situation, it became essential that she keep her eye on what she hoped to achieve, and not be derailed by the daily frustrations and privation. This is the difference between acting and reacting. In order to ensure that we would be ready when my father came to find us—and she never doubted that he would—she had to refuse all offers of help in exchange for marriage. This is an example of her acting in a way that supported her ultimate goal.

She could have chosen, instead, to react to the hopelessness that was all around us, to the starvation that stared us in the face every day. She could have accepted one of the many marriage proposals she received and we would have been taken care of in the short term, yes, but we would never have been able to leave Siberia. Once you married a Russian, you became Russian in the eyes of the state, and you were not allowed to leave. I am very grateful to my mother for keeping her eye every day on her ultimate goal—leaving Siberia with my father, with our family reunited.

Once we make up our minds to *act* and not to simply *react*, limitless possibilities open up before us. This is true in all situations—even the ones that appear hopeless at first blush. It is also a concept that I must often spend time working on with patients before any real progress can be made. Many are the people in this world who do not think before they act, and whose actions are really only reactions to the actions of others. I've found that this compulsion to react immediately can often be the entire source of difficulty for certain individuals.

I once had a patient who spent far too much of his life worrying. "Patrick" was paralyzed by the "what ifs" in his life. What if he lost his job? What if his wife left him? What if his kids became disobedient? What if he became sick? As we talked, it became clear that none of these things seemed likely to happen, and yet he spent many hours worrying that they might. He was essentially *reacting* to imaginary scenarios even before any external actions occurred.

My homework for Patrick, as an accompaniment to our therapy sessions, was to have him write each of his fears on a page in a spiral notebook. Then he was to calmly list the many possible actions he could take, should the worst come to pass. I stressed that it was a hypothetical exercise, and as such should not create more stress. He experienced some difficulty with this homework at first, but after he learned to address his fears head-on, he began to feel much less fear in his life.

I then encouraged Patrick to make another list—a list of the ways in which he could act right now to ensure that those feared events did *not* occur. He could volunteer for an important project at work, he could take his wife out to dinner once a week, and so on. Within a few weeks of doing this exercise, Patrick found that putting his fears on paper diminished their power over him. It also gave him a focus on what he could do to make positive changes and avert the negative outcomes that he had previously been sitting around waiting to be realized. By troubleshooting in advance and making a written list of possible actions for him to take, Patrick brought his fears under control.

Instead of giving knee-jerk reactions to our external circumstances, if we take the time to think ahead to our desired outcome and look deep inside ourselves to see how we can increase our motivation toward that desired outcome, we can become quietly unstoppable—like my mother. With love and inspiration, it's difficult to go wrong.

My mother was motivated by the most basic instinct of motherhood: survival of her offspring. She did everything she could to ensure that we would survive, and yet through all the struggles she never lost sight of her own moral compass. She did what she had to do, but she did it with compassion, persistence, gratitude, and loving-kindness. My mother believed in the value of kindness—to her loved ones, herself, and the rest of the world—and so was motivated to teach us one of the most basic but important life skills we would ever learn: to look deep inside and (despite the hardship) find a way to be kind.

12.

Be Kind

Each person has inside a basic decency and goodness.
If he listens to it and acts on it, he is giving a great deal
of what it is the world needs most. It is not complicated,
but it takes courage for a person to listen to
his own good.

—PABLO CASALS

IN A HUT on the other side of the village, a mother prepared her young child Sascha to brave the darkness and
cross the village on a surreptitious errand.

"You must run," the mother told her son. "And if anyone speaks to you, do not tell them what you are doing. If
they watch you to see where you go, come home instead."

"Yes, Mama." The boy trembled at the prospect of what
he was about to do. Everyone in the village knew that villagers were not supposed to offer help to the newcomers
who had been dumped there on Stalin's orders. But Sascha's
mother had seen the thin children in the street. She had
seen the mother working hard every day and still holding

her head up high. As a mother herself, she could not watch the family starve and do nothing to help.

And the old grandmother—the one the little boys called Babcia—had even helped Sascha's family once. She had known the right plant to boil and paste on Sascha's chest for a cough so bad that he could hardly breathe. The old woman had brought Sascha's mother the root and in her limited Russian told her how to prepare it.

So Sascha's mother buttoned her son's coat up high, put a carrot in one pocket and an onion in the other, and the child set out to make his way to the hut where he knew the two little boys lived.

Meanwhile, Zosia had used the last cup of flour to make a thin gruel that she cooked in a pan as flatbread. There was only enough for one, which they split four ways. It sat warmly in the stomach, even if it was tasteless and unsatisfying going down.

"My tummy wants more," said Jurek.

"Have a sip of water," said his mother, lifting his cup.

"There is no more bread?"

"I'm sorry, Jurek. The flour is all gone."

At that moment, there was a light rap upon the door of the hut. The two women exchanged glances, then Zosia moved across the floor and opened the door. A young boy from across the village stood there in the dim light, nervously shuffling his feet. He thrust a hand into each pocket and held a carrot and an onion out before him. He turned his head to glance into the darkness on either side of him. "Take them," he whispered.

Zosia lifted the produce from his hands and the child shot off into the darkness. "*Spasiba*," she called quietly to his retreating back.

I REMEMBER THIS young boy who delivered occasional bits of food to our hut after dark. We did not know his family, but they were kind to us. And we could never show our thanks because the villagers were told that we were to be considered enemies of the state and should not be helped. They would have been disciplined for helping us, had others found out. This always struck me as a double act of kindness on their part—one for wanting to help, and another for braving the risk associated with helping. Like those who ran the Underground Railroad to help American slaves find freedom, or the citizens in Germany who hid Jews during the Holocaust, this family put themselves at risk to help us and we were very grateful.

My mother was always torn when she received such gifts, both because of the sacrifice it represented to the family giving them, and also because she could not adequately acknowledge the kindness. The best she could do was to tell the young boy, "*Spasiba*" (thank you), as he ran away. She always hoped her thanks got back to the boy's mother, but we never knew.

Oddly enough, there was an unspoken rule that niceties such as kindness and manners were discouraged by the Communist government, and not just to people like us who were "enemies of the state." There was a general feeling in that place and at that time, that such traits as manners belonged to the bourgeois, to the cultured middle class, and so were to be rejected. The proletariat, the working-class peasants, were seen as the future of Communism, and anything middle class was suspect. This attitude was very difficult for my family to adopt, as they had always held pleasantries and manners in high esteem, and yet we did not want to draw attention to ourselves as being among the intelligentsia or the bourgeois. To do so was too dangerous a distinction to make, and so we learned to hide that aspect of our lives.

To me that seems an inestimably sad part of the whole experience of Siberia—to have had to hide a tendency toward kindness, especially in a place that would have been so much more tolerable if people had simply been kind to one another. Fortunately, there *were* kind people who risked a great deal to show us kindness, knowing that not only would they get nothing in return, but that they could even be punished if their actions on our behalf were discovered. To this day, that seems to me to be the ultimate triumph of human spirit over circumstances.

Despite the difficulties we experienced in Siberia, I believe that people are basically good and decent and kind. I also believe that the possibilities for showing kindness to others are limitless. Today most of us are fortunate to live in a world where kindness is accepted and even rewarded. I would also wager that most of us can't fully grasp what a world without kindness would look like. Having lived in Siberia, where kindness was a covert act of defiance, if it was practiced at all, I can tell you that kindness is a virtue that we must work to uphold if we hope to survive as a species. A world with no kindness is not a pretty world.

There is a Buddhist saying: "If you light a lamp for someone else, it will also brighten your path." Being kind to others not only makes the world a little bit more livable for all of us, it also makes *you* feel better about yourself. And kind people are more likely to be on the receiving end of kindness. That sounds like the ultimate in a win-win proposition, wouldn't you agree?

Deeds of kindness are the outward display of kindness, but kindness cannot only be defined in terms of our actions. Cultivating our inner kindness—in thoughts and gentle feelings toward others—is equally important as our outward shows of kindness. In order to be truly kind, we need to be aware of our thoughts as well—thoughts regarding others, and thoughts regarding ourselves. If you find yourself judging the actions of others, or even berating yourself for some imperfection, you are not practicing kindness. Lao Tzu, the Chinese philosopher and father of Taoism, wrote, "Kindness in words creates confidence. Kindness in thinking creates profoundness. Kindness in feeling creates love."

It is important to remember that in order to practice loving-kindness, we must not forget to be kind to ourselves. Say, for example, that you forget that it is best to own your emotions and so you lash out at another. You can always revisit the moment later and replay how you would have behaved differently. You can analyze where things went wrong and make a plan for doing better in the future. You can also take the opportunity to apologize to the person you wounded and let them know that you are working on responding in a more constructive way. And once you have done that, you should take a moment to pat yourself on the back—for in noticing that you have failed, and setting it to rights, you take the first step in succeeding. Never see failure as an end. It is always a beginning—a chance to learn from our mistakes and do things better the next time.

AT FIRST ZOSIA was relieved when the commissar told her that she would no longer be working in the barn with the cows. The large animals had truly terrified her, and the combination of feeding, watering, herding, and milking had taken more energy than she was bringing into her body with food. Work with the cows—combined with her body's attempts to overcome the effects of a nasty recurring bout of typhus—had made each day a struggle against exhaustion.

So she was relieved, yet also concerned, because after the commissar relieved her of her work burden, he told her that her family would soon be relocated. No explanation was given beyond the same tired phrase the Russian soldiers had used when deporting them from Poland: "Stalin has allowed that you should be moved to better living conditions." The irony of such words was almost too much to take. *So forgive me*, thought Zosia, *if I do not believe it.*

How would they manage, starting over in a new village? No one would know them there. And what about her payment of a weekly loaf of bread? Although a loaf of bread a week had been precious little for a family of four, it had at least been one additional tiny step between them and starvation. And now that would be gone, too. How would her family fill the void? Already her sons had become so thin that their skin looked like a sheet of paper wrapped around their bones. How much more could her children lose before they succumbed to starvation?

Would they have a better hut in the new place? Or worse? Would she be given even more difficult work than the tending of cows? There were so many unknowns to ponder, but Zosia did her best to put the worry aside and focus on the day-to-day.

The night before they were to set out for the new village, a knock came upon the door of their hut. When Zosia opened the door, Marya stood there in the darkness. She held a heavy burden cradled in the folds of her skirt.

"Good evening," Zosia said in her limited Russian, trying to hide her surprise.

"The cows are missing you," said Marya with a twinkle in her eye. "And as they were being milked tonight, they said that I should bring you this." She held up a jar of clear liquid.

"And this is water?" Babcia asked, having come to stand behind her daughter as she answered the door.

"Shh, Mama," Zosia said, not wanting to seem ungrateful. "It is the whey. What is left behind after the curds are pulled for cheese." Zosia knew that whey was full of vitamins and protein. "*Spasiba*," she said as she accepted the jar. The boys came forward, too, curious to see.

Marya retrieved a second quart jar from her skirts. She handed that one to Babcia.

"Yes," said Marya. "And the state tells me that I am to feed this whey to the pigs with their slops" She handed another jar to Andrew, and a fourth to Jurek. "But I am thinking—and the cows agree—that the pigs will not notice the difference if tonight their whey is water."

"Tell the cows *spasiba*, too," said Zosia, and she curtsied with a smile in her eyes.

I OFTEN WONDER whether we were told we would be moved to a new village because word had reached someone in charge that my father had joined the British forces and would soon be looking for us. Were we supposed to be living in better conditions when he found us? Or were they moving us farther away, hoping he would not be able to find us? There is no way to know, of course, all these years hence, but still, I wonder. It is an example of the sort of Big Brother paranoia that Stalin's government bred—much as George Orwell described in his book *1984*.

Even after we were relocated to America and had lived there for years, my mother would not give an interview to an American reporter to describe our ordeal in Siberia. Stalin's reach was too long for her to feel comfortable. But my grandmother, ever the rebel, gave her own interview in 1951 because, she said, she had no fear. I believe her.

Fortunately for us, even in the midst of an unfeeling system that treated *us* like cattle, there were individuals like Marya who believed in our humanity and cared enough to risk their own positions to offer us aid. Albert Schweitzer wrote, "Sometimes our light goes out but is blown into a flame by another human being. Each of us owes deepest thanks to those who have rekindled this light." Marya's kindness did this. She fed our bodies but also rekindled our spirits, and in the midst of all that suffering, it was a balm to be treated with kindness and compassion.

Years later, when I had the opportunity to read *The Diary of Anne Frank*, I marveled at how simply and directly she expressed this notion when she wrote, "How wonderful it is that nobody need wait a single minute before starting to improve the world." Her eloquence and wisdom in the face of suffering has stayed with me for years.

Having spent a lifetime trying to understand and help others, I have come to the conclusion that kindness is the quality I most admire in my friends, coworkers, patients and even strangers. I agree with the novelist Henry James, who said, "Three things in human life are important. The first is to be kind. The second is to be kind. And the third is to be kind."

The best, most effective psychotherapists and counselors always operate from a place of kindness. Kindness is also a spiritual act. Each of the world's major religions espouses kindness in their sacred texts. His Holiness the Dalai Lama has said, "My religion is very simple. My religion is kindness." And the beauty of kindness is that it isn't difficult, and the smallest gesture can make a vast improvement in the situation of another.

The good news is that anyone can be kind at any time. You need not be in a position of power to show kindness to others. Aesop wrote a fable in which a mighty lion catches a tiny mouse. When the mouse begs to be spared, the lion lets him go free; the mouse tells him that one day, he will repay his kindness. The lion laughs. What can a tiny mouse do for a mighty lion? But sure enough, one day, the lion becomes trapped in a rope snare and cannot free himself. Along comes the mouse and chews the rope, setting the lion free. The moral at the end is, "No act of kindness, no matter how small, is ever wasted."

Being kind to your enemies or your oppressors can also produce surprising results. I am convinced that because of my family's civil and kind attitude and behavior we were treated more kindly than we would have been otherwise. "Tenderness and kindness," wrote Khalil Gibran, "are not signs of weakness and despair, but manifestations of strength and resolution."

In my work with some of the most severely disturbed patients, I noticed something startling. As each one of them progressed in their therapy, two human qualities emerged before any others, and these qualities signified the approach of a great breakthrough. Those qualities were kindness and a sense of humor. When one of my severely disturbed patients learned to laugh, or even make a joke, I knew that we had made incredible progress and that even more success would follow. Laughter was always a very hopeful sign. And once that same individual initiated even the smallest act of kindness—not at my urging, mind you, but completely on his or her own—then I knew we had truly embarked on a path to concluding a successful round of therapy.

Do you remember Nancy, the woman prone to angry outburst that made no sense, and who had been placed in a back ward for hopeless cases? Well, as discussed before, active listening encouraged her to begin to respond and verbalize in ways that made sense. And once she began to make sense, others responded to her in increasingly positive ways. And once others began to respond to Nancy, I noted her human kindness returning. At first it was a simple "thank you" that surprised her caregivers as they extended Nancy the simple daily assistance of helping her dress—the kind of assistance that had gone unacknowledged for years. That "thank you" opened the way for more and greater acts of civility and kindness on Nancy's part, and surely played a tremendous role in her ultimate release and assignment to a loving home care environment.

There was a bumper sticker popular in the 1990s that read, "Practice random acts of kindness and senseless acts of beauty." This is an inspired way to take a negative phrase—a phrase that expressed violence and cruelty—and rework it to suit the cause of kindness and compassion. And we can do this not only with words but also in our deeds. As many survivors of trial and suffering have said before, and as the notion of radical gratitude expresses, we *can* make good from the bad. In a sense, that is what I am doing here, for you. Taking the early bad in my life and transforming it to good for others.

And we need not think of kindness only in terms of the big differences we can make. Small acts of kindness ripple outward and increase as they go. The smallest and simplest act of kindness that we can all practice—whenever we encounter another person—is a smile. A smile costs nothing. It is easy to give, it makes you feel better in the giving, and a smile is contagious. "Smile at each other," said Mother Teresa, "smile at your wife, smile at your husband, smile at your children, smile at each other—it doesn't matter who it is—and that will help you to grow up in greater love for each other."

A smile is a kindness that expresses love; it reaches out like a hand to others, costs nothing, and even makes you feel better in the process. A smile is the best sort of contagion. So remember to take a moment to smile and spread your kindness to others. Kindness is a balm that soothes away pain, and a smile is the quickest way to express kindness.

Fortunately, being kind to others is also good for the self. Those people who make it a point to be kind to others are more likely to be happy and well adjusted themselves. And perhaps more attractive, too. When asked for beauty tips, the actress Audrey Hepburn is said to have answered, "For attractive lips, speak words of kindness."

A smile or a kind word is also the quickest way to show forgiveness. And forgiveness is healing. It is the ultimate act of kindness that we can extend to one another, and even to ourselves. We are all human. We will all fail on occasion. We will all disappoint those we love at some time in our lives. But forgiveness allows the slate to be wiped clean. It allows us to "move on" and move forward. Forgiveness heals more than just relationships. It heals our own souls and restores us to balance. And when we learn to recognize our feelings of hurt or anger and consciously "let go," we take the first step in finding peace.

13.

To Find Peace, Let Go

To be wronged is nothing unless you continue
to remember it.

—CONFUCIUS

OUT ON THE plain, the family prepared to spend the night.
Along with another group of refugees, they were being relocated to another camp. They did not know why, but they
knew by now not to question it. It was a warm summer night
and the people well enough to walk had traveled many miles
that day. Fatigue showed in their bodies as they searched for
a place on the ground to make a modest bedroll and pass
the night.

Babcia's age qualified her to ride in the ox-driven cart
along with little Jurek, and that is where they also slept. Andrew and his mother found a spot beneath the oxcart, and
Zosia rolled up their extra clothing to fashion a long pil-

low for the two of them to share. As the air cooled around them, Zosia pulled up closer to her son, put an arm over his shoulders and breathed in his boyish scent. Motherly feelings swelled in her heart—she would protect him with her life if need be.

But tonight that would not be necessary, so Zosia slept.

The night was clear and peaceful, and despite the aching muscles in his legs, Andrew lay awake for a long time after darkness fell. He stared into the vast and beautiful nighttime sky. The stars were so thick above him! And so far away that he felt smaller, even, than his seven years of age.

As the sound of peaceful breathing began all around him, the rising, high-pitched howling of a wolf began in the distance. His mother, already asleep, clutched him tighter in her dreams. The long winters had taught Andrew that the presence of wolves was a cause for fear. And yet something had been shifting in his mind when he thought of wolves. Summer, the villagers taught him, was not a time to fear wolves. In the summertime, wolves are well fed and happy. They are raising families far from the village, and humans do not interest wolves.

So instead, Andy listened to the wolves as if they were singing a song. Each wolf had his part and each took up before the other left off, so that a continuous chorus of wolf voices surrounded him out there on the plain. As far as he knew, everyone else in camp was asleep, and the wolves sang for him alone.

In the midst of their singing, Andy thought of his grandfather. He remembered how fiercely and lovingly his grandfather had held on to him when they were loaded onto the train. He remembered how easily his Dziadek had given up food, saying he was not hungry, so the children could have more. He remembered how wolves had killed a calf and left it for his starving family to find.

As his mother held him in her sleep, and a sleepy body in the cart above them rustled into a better position, Andy stared up at the night sky, listening to the music of the wolves and letting it lull him to sleep.

THAT SUMMER EVENING, listening to the wolves calling to one another, remains one of the most peaceful images that I hold in my heart. I can remember it and be transported back to that warm night sky peppered with stars so close it felt as if I might reach up and touch them. I remember the comfort that I felt, the closeness to my grandfather that I sensed out there on the steppe. To this day, that night feeds my soul.

That night on the plain also marks a pivotal moment in my life. It was a time when I let go of my fear of wolves

and instead felt a connection to all the earth and its creatures. Recognizing our connectedness is both a spiritual
and a meditative exercise. Aristotle said, "In all things of
nature there is something of the marvelous." The wolves
were certainly marvelous that night. My mother, too, loved
and celebrated nature. Throughout her life, she strived to
impart this love of nature to others, and I am grateful. I
know my own love for nature helped me to survive Siberia,
taught me to trust and believe in the rightness of the world,
and continues to give me joy every day of my life. Nature is
a great stress reliever.

Stress, particularly as a source of illness, is rampant in our
modern world. Many people complain of being under too
much stress. They have stressful jobs, their lives are stressful, and they want help. For over thirty years, I have taught
stress reduction, and I can tell you this: It's not a problem
that's going away any time soon.

Stress affects our relationships and our performance
on the job, and it prevents us from enjoying all the simple
things in life, such as good food, music, lively and meaningful conversation—even sleep. What's ironic, though, is
that it's the only major ill of our times over which we have
complete control.

Whether you want to lower stress levels in your own life
or be of help to others who wish to ameliorate stress, it is

necessary first to understand a little bit about stress. Stress, by psychological definition, is a state of mental or emotional strain or suspense, caused by a reaction to events happening around us. It is rarely caused by the events themselves, but rather is a function of how we respond to them, how we perceive and handle those events.

When people talk about experiencing stress because of their families, their jobs, or their finances, they always think of the stress as coming from "out there." In reality, the stress we put on ourselves (with our thinking, interpretations, and expectations) is what causes the negative stress response. Reactions such as elevated heart rate, high blood pressure, shallow breathing, tension headaches—these are all things we create for ourselves. If you work to change your thinking, change your attitude, and change your philosophy, you can do away with most major causes of stress. "If you are distressed by anything external," wrote Marcus Aurelius, a Roman emperor and Stoic philosopher, "the pain is not due to the thing itself, but to your estimate of it; and this you have the power to revoke at any moment."

As a young witness to the terrifying incident of the Russian soldier ordering my grandmother to pray at gunpoint, I learned early on that the ability to de-stress a charged situation would be key to my survival. In fact, the skill of deescalating tension is one of the greatest lessons I've taken from my time in Siberia. This is an ability that we all have within us, and it can serve us well if we only let it.

In the late 1970s, I lived alone in an apartment in downtown Buffalo, New York, in an unsafe neighborhood. One day I decided to take the day off from work. While showering, I heard two strange male voices having a discussion in my living room. My instinct told me I was being burglarized and that the two men assumed no one was home. Acting on a purely intuitive level, I wrapped a towel around my waist and walked out into the living room. I made sure not to get between the two very large men and the door (I wanted them to quite literally *see a way out*—any physical confrontation would have been foolish on my part), and I walked out with a smile on my face. In a very relaxed manner I asked, "Oh, what are you guys doing here?"

They were surprised to see me, but clearly also wanted to avoid trouble and after a pause said, "Isn't this where we were supposed to move the piano?"

I said, "No. I think you have the wrong place. It must be next door."

Then they meekly walked out of the apartment and drove away in a truck that was parked outside. You can call it depolarizing, deescalating, or defusing a situation, but it is a skill that we all have dormant within us. We just need to have the confidence to bring it out when it's needed.

Another story I like to tell my clients is about the tough-guy actor who, whenever he walked into a bar, seemed always to be accosted by drunks wanting to fight him. He learned to approach each belligerent fellow and say, "Hey, I don't want to fight you, I want to have a drink with you!" Thus the situation immediately deescalated, and the would-be macho contestants turned into meek and mild fans, thrilled to be sitting and having a drink with a famous movie star.

Meditation is an ancient and very effective method of reducing tension and stress in people's lives. Westerners can sometimes find meditation difficult because they have not learned how to relax on their own, so about ten years ago, I started teaching both relaxation and meditation in the same course.

When the body is in a relaxed state, the mind also relaxes. It's nearly impossible to have fearful and stressful thoughts in a very relaxed body. Once you have learned how to relax your muscles, you have gained a skill that you can use any time you want to, even during situations that normally would produce a great amount of tension or stress.

Tension is the opposite of relaxation. The tension we carry in our bodies contributes a great deal to the stress we experience. Learning how to let go of this physical stress and tension is essential to relaxation.

Fortunately, we can actually *use* tension to create relaxation. The easiest muscles to start with are in the arms. First, sit in a chair and rest your arms comfortably. Then purposefully create tension in your arms by clenching your fists. Feel the tension build all the way to the shoulders in both arms. Hold it for ten seconds. Remember that the tension is there because you put it there. Then slowly release half of the tension from your arms. Take a slow deep breath and on the exhale release half again. Hold this quarter-tension for another five seconds and then exhale and let it all go.

The important concept here is *letting go*. You create tension, then you let it go. You are in control. You put the tension there, you control it, and you can let it go. Once the arms are mastered, do the same thing with the legs, then the stomach and pelvic area. Each time, use the same technique of tighten and release.

The tension that develops in our necks and faces often manifests itself as real pain. That old expression "he's a pain in the neck" is more than idle chatter. There are dozens of muscles in the face, more per square inch than in any other part of the body, and you can often see tension in the face, especially around the eyes and mouth. To relax your neck and face, pull your head toward your body and lift your shoulders; imagine a turtle pulling into its shell. Close your eyes and tighten them as much as you can. Feel the tension around your eyes as you do this. Do the same thing with your mouth. Press your lips together so you can feel the tension all around your lips and mouth. Combining the lips and the eyes together, your entire face should be tensed up. Hold it for five seconds and then follow the half-release sequence as described previously. If you find tension anywhere in the face, really concentrate on letting it go.

The more you practice these techniques, the more successful each session will be. But this is only the beginning. There's still more "letting go" to do.

ANDREW TOSSED RESTLESSLY in the new hut in the new village to which they had been relocated. He sought to find a comfortable spot on the thin blanket on which he slept. It was warm, and the late summer insects buzzed outside the door. His brother snored lightly beside him, but Andrew could not sleep. Each new position seemed to press against a different sore place on his body. And even an extra blanket underneath him did nothing to cushion his protruding hipbones and shoulder blades.

In addition to the physical discomfort, his mind kept delivering bad dreams. They had been happening more and more lately. He was tired, but the bed was not inviting because of what appeared before him when he closed his eyes. The dreams, when he awoke from them, kept him awake as he relived what he had seen.

The horrors he had seen in his young life were many, but ironically, it was not the horrors that were plaguing him. The dreams that he did not wish to keep reliving were dreams of food. Mountains of food appeared before him as he slept. He could smell the odors of the food before him, and they were heady. His mouth watered. He felt such a sense of longing.

The food had been a dream, but the disappointment, when he awoke, was real. Often there were tears on his face even before he was fully awake. It made him not want to go to sleep anymore.

Zosia, roused by her son's restlessness, turned to him and asked, "Andrew? Are you all right?"

"Yes, Mama."

"Why are you awake?"

"I'm not tired."

"It's the middle of the night, Andy. It is time to sleep."

"I don't like what I see when I sleep."

Zosia trembled to think what her son might be seeing in his dreams. She knew the heartlessness and violence that plagued her nightmares, and she worried for what he might face when he closed his eyes. But she knew also that she must ask in order to help make it go away. "What do you see?"

"Food. I smell it, too." Tears began to slide down his cheeks. "And then I wake up."

"And there is no food," said Zosia, suddenly understanding, tears filling her own eyes.

"I know it's okay," he said. "But I don't want to go back to sleep."

Zosia wondered what she could do to help her son. "Sleep is important for your body, Andy. If we could make the food dreams stop, would you try to sleep again? Could you do that for me?"

He nodded.

"Well, here is what I need you to do. When you start to dream about food again, tell yourself—your dreaming self—that you don't want to see it anymore. Then tell yourself to dream about a favorite place, a secret place that is just for you. Do you know a secret place?"

He thought of the tree across the stream. The tree with the low branches that he could climb all the way to the top of and see across the plain for miles. "Yes, my favorite place is—"

"Shh." She put a finger to his lips. "Don't tell. It's your secret. But try to go to sleep thinking about your favorite place. And when you dream and you start to see the food, walk away from it and go to your favorite place."

MY MOTHER TAUGHT me that I could direct my dreams to stop going where I did not want them to go. And in the years since then, I have used that principle in other aspects of my life as well. If I find myself slipping into certain mental states that contribute to tension (unpleasant memories, fears, guilt, resentments, etc.) I will often simply command the thoughts to go away. I find it helpful to address myself directly, saying, "Andrew, let go of that." This can be a very effective affirmation—and easy to remember, too!

It is not just our bodies that need to spend time relaxing. Our minds need relaxing as well. Practicing *mindfulness* encourages relaxation. By mindfulness I mean a state of mind in which we are focused solely on the present moment. One lighthearted restating of the concept of mindfulness could be the old adage, "Wherever you go, there you are."

When in a state of mindfulness, whatever thoughts or memories come to the mind are acknowledged, observed, and then "let go." When we are in a state of mindfulness, regrets, anxieties, and anger lose their hold on us because we are free to simply note the emotions that surface and then move on.

Stress and fear come from a preoccupation with the past and the future. You can reduce stress in your life simply by spending more time in the present and practicing mindfulness. To help my patients visualize the concept of mindfulness, I tell them to take a moment and imagine themselves in a room that is totally dark. To get rid of the dark, you can try physically casting it aside with your hands, but no matter how hard you flail against darkness, you will not move it away. You cannot fight and destroy darkness. There is only one way to banish darkness, and that is to let in the light. Mindfulness lets in the light. It hastens en*light*enment.

We take a big step toward enlightenment when we come to understand that we cannot go back and change the past, but we can always go forward and change the future. Such focus on the present is a way of *letting in the light* and casting away the helpless feelings that cause much of our day-to-day stress.

Remember, you can always have a less stressful future by making changes today, by altering your *now*.

These days, it's all too easy to succumb to the lure of the myriad electronic gadgets that vie for our attention. Between our cell phones, pagers, and e-mail, we are rarely—if ever—unreachable. But as Jon Kabat-Zinn (best known for teaching mindfulness as a way to overcome stress) asks, "In a world where we can be in touch with anyone at any time, have we lost touch with ourselves?"

Visualization can help us to get back in touch with our lost selves. Visualization is when you imagine a picture in your mind—either of what you want to happen, or what you wish to cast away. One of my favorite visualizations involves imagining a scene that will rid our minds of negative thoughts. If we practice this specific way of letting go (releasing anxieties, resentments, and worries), we can soon be rid of the negative states of mind that unhealthily preoccupy us. I tell my patients (or myself!) the following:

Close your eyes and picture yourself sitting at the edge of a stream. It's a beautiful, peaceful summer afternoon, and you are alone with nature. A soft breeze rustles through the trees. Light sparkles off the water as it ripples past you, close enough to touch. High, billowy clouds move across the sky; flowers tip their heads toward the sun.

Now imagine you can hear water moving over the stones, the echo of faraway birdcalls, a sigh as the wind moves through the trees. Then feel the breeze: slightly cool, refreshing; it lifts your hair. Lightly play your fingers across the water to touch the satiny coolness. Smell the air: the new-mown hay of a distant field, the heady scent of honeysuckle climbing a forgotten fencepost. Take the time to make everything as real as possible in your mind.

Then imagine a small wooden box sitting on your lap. The box is open. In your mind's eye identify those things you want to let go of. They could be worries, fears, hatreds, anxieties, bad memories, whatever you'd like to release in order to feel more relaxed and peaceful.

Now remove each of those things from your mind in the form of little pebbles, and put them, one at a time, into the box. Identify each one as you place it there. When you have put everything you want to be rid of into the box, close the lid and gently place the box into the stream in front of you. See it bob up and down in the water? Watch the current catch it and slowly carry it away. Don't take your eyes off the box. Keep watching it bobbing in the stream, getting smaller as it floats away from you into the distance, until you cannot see it anymore. After it has disappeared, continue enjoying the scenery for a few more moments, then open your eyes and return to your everyday life, your emotional burdens lightened.

In my efforts to help people, I often explore their openness to meditation. For many of my clients, traditional meditation does not suit their temperament. If they are action oriented, and sitting still is difficult for them, they are often surprised to learn that some of the things they do already are a form of meditation. Like sitting very quietly in a forest, or on the beach, or mountaintop, feeling very calm and peaceful. Some runners enter into a meditative state while running. Certain types of music will put people into a meditative frame of mind. Likewise, the total absorption of prayer.

In each case, two factors are at play: relaxation, and focus on the present. During meditation we focus our attention on our inner wisdom, calmness, and creativity, which does not exist in the past or future, but only now.

Meditation relies on stillness and silence, which is something sorely lacking in modern life. In this twenty-first-century world, we are continually bombarded with sound—traffic, television, loud music, public address systems, even other people's cell phone conversations. Many people have become uncomfortable with silence and will turn on the radio or the television simply to have some noise, some *company,* as one client of mine put it. But Psalm 46:10 reads, "Be still, and know that I am God." It is in this stillness that one gets in touch with spirituality, inner wisdom, and, ultimately, God.

If prayer is *talking* to God, then meditation is *listening* to God.

If we sit in silence, we tune in to nature, to the elements, and to our own intuitions and inner wisdom. And we must cultivate this silence away from the noisy world in which we live.

Silence gives us a new outlook on everything. We need silence in our lives in order to reach others, to help others. Those of us who are committed to helping others must foster this silence. For stillness and meditation nourish our souls in the same way that food and water nourish our bodies. This is how we take care of ourselves, so that we are then able to help others.

Mahatma Gandhi said, "In the attitude of silence the soul finds the path in a clearer light, and what is elusive and deceptive resolves itself into crystal clearness."

So I urge you: learn to relax and meditate in whatever form works for you. If necessary, take some classes, read some books, practice. And learn to sit in silence for a portion of every day. In stillness you gain important access to feelings and thoughts that might otherwise have stayed hidden. Once you access your inner wisdom, life will become richer, more enjoyable, and more meaningful. Deep meditation is a form of love—love of self, of others, and of the world as a whole. And nothing heals better than love.

14.

Love Is the Opposite of Fear

It is not how much we give, but how much love we put
into giving.

—MOTHER TERESA

IN THE SPRING of 1942, Hitler's army invaded Russia.
As Stalin began losing that war, he grew desperate for help
from the West. Under pressure from the Allies and the Polish government-in-exile (located in England), Stalin agreed
to release the Polish troops he was holding, and their families. The Allies needed as many able-bodied men as possible, and Vincent Bienkowski suddenly became more valuable as a soldier than as a prisoner-of-war. The men locked
away in Stalin's prisons and gulags could, Stalin realized, be
conscripted to help in the fight against the Nazis.

Shortly after his release, Andrew's father began the search for
his wife and the rest of his banished family. Vincent set out—in

a British military transport vehicle—to find his wife and sons somewhere in the vast wasteland of Siberia. Exhausted and starving, but excited by the possibility of seeing his family again, he set out with a worn photograph and a great deal of hope. He followed the route of the railway train that had carried deportees away. At each village along the way, he stopped and asked after his family. His questions were mostly greeted with blank stares, sometimes even with open hostility, but still he continued on, driving ever farther into the Siberian wasteland.

After three weeks of searching, he finally happened on a village where a picture of Babcia led a toothless old woman to describe a fortune-teller who had helped many people, and her daughter who tended to the village cows. Although doubtful that the women described could possibly be his dignified mother-in-law and educated, refined wife (Vincent was certain his wife would not be one to tend cows), he had told himself that he would explore every lead, no matter how slight the chance for success.

"Can you tell me where I can find these women?" Vincent asked the old woman. "Perhaps one of them can help me find my family."

"Ask the fortune-teller." The old woman's eyes gleamed. "She is wise. She told me of a plant that could help my rheumatism—her husband had it, you know. Suffered terribly, he did. And she would make him—"

"Yes, but," he interrupted. "I'm sorry. The directions? It is urgent that I find my family."

"Oh, you will not find them here," said the old woman chewing at her toothless gums. "They are gone."

"Gone?" Vincent's heart sank. He hardly dared to ask. "Dead?"

The old woman laughed as if he'd told a fine joke. When she caught her breath, she said, "They didn't leave here dead—though that child was terrible skinny—but not dead, no. Relocated."

"Relocated?" he asked. "When? What for?"

"Who knows what for. For the state. We do not question. Last fall, I believe it was. Or maybe spring. Into summer, even. But I'm sure it wasn't winter. I'd remember if it was winter."

Vincent told himself to be patient. The information he needed would come if he could just stand and listen.

"Sometimes there's a new village starting up and they need workers to build it. Sometimes there's a skill needed and they'll move the whole family. Nobody knows why, but they go. Oh, they go all right." She cackled some more.

"Can you tell me where the village is?"

She looked at him for a long, hard minute. "That way," she said, pointing into the setting sun.

And so Vincent followed the old woman's finger to the

next village west, then the next, and the next. The weather had warmed since the start of his journey and the going was easier. At the third village, he was given directions to a small hut at the outskirts where he was told a young Polish family had been the newest arrivals.

As he neared the hut, he saw a woman sweeping the yard with a worn-down broom made of bundled grasses. The bones of her elbows stuck out from her thin forearms and her hipbones protruded even from the folds of her skirt. These poor people were so abysmally thin, he thought. Had no one escaped suffering at Stalin's hand? The woman's hair was long and neatly wound into a bun. A glance told him she could not be his wife, but perhaps she would know Zosia, or would have seen her, and she could give him a little more hope to keep looking.

He approached her as she swept and cleared his throat. "Pardon me," he said in Polish and the woman spun around to face him. They stared at one another for a long moment.

"Vincent? Is it you?" Zosia asked this thin man in a British uniform before her. His eyes, so sad, yet so familiar. Could it be her husband? After all this time? Were her hunger and fatigue playing tricks on her?

The man smiled and came forward. Her eyes filled with tears. Then Vincent put his arms around her and lifted her from the ground. She laughed as he spun her around. Her body was so light; she weighed so little that it pained him, even in this moment of great joy.

And then Zosia knew that this man who hugged her was her husband and he had come—at last—to find them—at last—and take them away from Siberia—at last! Tears fell down her cheeks as she cried and laughed and hugged her husband. She called to the children inside the hut. But they had already heard the commotion and emerged, thin shoulders poking through their too large shirts.

"Andrew, Jurek, look who has come! It is your papa! He has found us!"

The two boys stared for a moment and then rushed forward to hug the laughing man's knees.

Miraculously, he had not only found them but had brought official papers from the Russian government that secured their release. He had brought a motorized vehicle—a truck with a covered bed—and a motorized vehicle was something the family had not seen for years.

When it came time to leave, Babcia was surprised at her hesitation. She had no love for this place, had dreamed of the day she could leave, and yet here was where her husband had passed his final days, here was where they had struggled so hard together to live in spite of deprivation and sickness and hunger. An unfamiliar pain tugged at her. What of all the others left behind who could not leave?

Should she gather her things? And then Babcia thought, "Things? What things? I have nothing here worth keeping. Let me leave whatever I had to the poor souls who must stay." And so she put the hut behind her, and walked to the truck driven by her son-in-law who had come to save them all. She did not look back.

OVER THE YEARS, it was my grandmother who told most of the stories from Siberia. She went from fortune-teller to storyteller, and she kept our memories alive. She believed it was important to remember, to never forget what we had survived, the trials we had lived through. And she always believed it was the miracle of love that brought my father to us in Siberia.

Psychologists, psychiatrists, and social scientists seldom speak about love. They mention caring, empathy, compassion, nurturing, positive regard, understanding, and generosity. But somehow they don't seem comfortable with the word LOVE. Many people aren't.

After all, what *is* love? Love is difficult to define or even understand.

Perhaps it's easier to define what love is *not*. It is not the pull of attraction that men and women initially feel toward each other. What we call "falling in love" or "being in love" is mostly sexual attraction. But real, deep, abiding love is not the physical attraction that we feel toward another human being. It is not something that goes on and off like a light bulb. It is not even friendship, or obligation or a sense of duty. It is not parental instinct.

Much of what we *call* love is seen as a transaction: "I'll give you five oranges for your five apples." It's also conditional: "I'll be nice to you, provide you with a home, and in exchange I want you to cook for me and be sexually available and faithful. If you do not live up to my expectations, I will not love you anymore."

But love cannot be adequately defined with words or intellectual concepts. It is that part of an individual that has nothing to do with the head. Love comes from the heart, from the soul, from God. It is the opposite of the "me first" modern ideology. It is those moments in which we let go of selfishness that we feel real love in our hearts.

Real love is unconditional. We understand this, but it's very difficult to put unconditional love into practice. As Gerald G. Jampolsky, author of *Love Is Letting Go of Fear*, says, "Evaluating and being evaluated by others, a habit from the past, results at worst in fear and at best in *conditional* love. To experience *unconditional* love, we must get rid of the evaluator, we need to hear our strong inner voice saying to ourselves and to others, 'I totally love and accept you as you are.'"

Unconditional love is a challenging concept and a tall order. For many of us, we may not be ready yet to love unconditionally. But we can still strive to make our love as unconditional as possible.

Early in my career, much of my work with patients was guided by what I learned in graduate school. As I look back now, I see I was working *from my head*. Gradually, as the years went by, I learned to work *from my heart*. Today, I firmly believe that to be truly helpful to others, working from the heart is essential. You don't give up your book knowledge; just allow your heart to have predominance. Love comes from the heart, not from the head. That is why it's so hard to understand love intellectually.

One of the most important truths I have learned in my work is this: *love is the opposite of fear*. I am always amazed that this concept is so very foreign to most people. In forty years of working with troubled individuals, I have learned that at the bottom of most problems lies fear. And fear keeps us from love, which we all need.

Here is a typical course in psychotherapy: Patient presents problems in relationships that cause a great deal of stress, dissatisfaction, resentment, and anger. Together we delve into the problems, digging deeper and deeper, until we arrive at the core. And this core is fear that exists, rarely at a conscious level. As we deal with this fear, understand it, resolve it, let it go, the other "problems" start gradually to disappear. Discover the deeply buried fear, deal with it, and the problems disappear. It sounds simple, and yet it can be so very difficult to accomplish.

"Mark" was a very unhappy man. He came to me in a desperate last-ditch attempt to straighten out his life. He had seriously considered suicide and wanted help. His marriage was falling apart. He had been fired from his job and was experiencing physical problems that were clearly caused by high levels of stress and anxiety. Mark and I hit it off right away and were quickly able to get to the root of his problem. Mark's troubles stemmed from an all-consuming fear of rejection and abandonment. Ironically, Mark spent so much time focused on the fear of his loved ones abandoning him, that his insecure actions began to push them away. In focusing so much on the fear, he was actually *creating* the very problem that he most feared would come to pass.

Once I got him to see this and recognize his own role, we began a series of therapeutic sessions in which Mark recounted instances in his childhood when he had felt abandoned. We dealt with them, resolved the feelings, and gradually Mark learned to view relationships with his wife and others in a less threatening way. With less fear and anxiety, he could see his relationships in a realistic light and interact with love instead of fear. Within three months, Mark reported a significant improvement in all his relationships and especially his marriage. After fifteen months, most of his physical problems had disappeared and he was dealing with life in a more relaxed and comfortable manner.

An excellent way to eliminate fear from your life—and a technique that Mark and I employed to great effect—is to ask yourself the question: "What would be the worst possible thing that could happen to me?" Close your eyes and imagine this terrible situation. Make it as real as you can, and as terrible as it could possibly be. Feel all of the emotions as they arise. Allow yourself to express those emotions in any way that is natural to you: crying, yelling, hitting a pillow, vocalizing them, whatever works for you. Keep doing this until there are no feelings left. Recognize that the fear within you has diminished—or even disappeared. Your final step is to take a moment and allow a feeling of relaxation and peace to flow over you. This is the absence of fear. Feels good, doesn't it?

There are many books about relationships that focus on how to "get" the love you need, and how to "keep" the love you have. But we should also ask, "How do I become a more loving human being?" In my experience, this is the question that gives direction and meaning to life.

Individuals who are guided by love are far happier than those who allow fear to drive their decisions. As a psychotherapist, teacher, and trainer, I emphasize love as a route to overcoming fear. And lives that are lived with a focus on love are simply more rich, full, and satisfying.

In Siberia, no matter how bad the situation was, we felt loved and safe within the family circle. We loved each other, and we were dedicated to helping each other survive. My grandparents' and my mother's courage, and their faith in our ultimate survival, were quite remarkable, especially in contrast to the overwhelming sense of defeat and hopelessness that existed all around us. And so, from inhospitable, desolate Siberia, I learned that love, courage, and faith can and do defeat fear.

Balzac said: "Love is, to the moral nature, exactly what the sun is to the earth." Strive to become more loving and you will find that you become less fearful, more likely to reach out spontaneously to those in need.

Avoidance is a clear indication of fear. And the more you avoid whatever thing you are afraid of, the stronger the fear will get. The best way to decrease fear is to face it. If you can approach and even embrace that which you are afraid of, the fear decreases. Overcoming fear can be taken in as small steps as needed. You may have heard the term "systematic desensitization." Systematic desensitization is a system of reducing fear, by means of gradually increasing exposure to that which creates the fear.

Thirty-five years ago, my son developed a strong fear of dogs. After trying all manner of calm explaining—none of which worked—I offered him a nickel each time he would stand near a dog. He liked money, and so, although it was difficult, he forced himself to stand by dogs in order to earn nickels. Soon, it was easy for him to stand next to a dog. After he had mastered that, he had to *touch* a dog to earn a nickel. Just a finger on the head would do. Again, after many nickels it became easy. Once that was achieved, he had to put his arms around a dog to earn a nickel. And so it went, until eventually his fear of dogs had completely disappeared. In the end, he even asked me to buy him a dog, which I did.

THE REUNITED FAMILY made their way to an Iranian refugee camp located just across the border of Russia and Iran. During the arduous trip, Andrew developed a fever that rose steadily. Zosia held his head in her lap throughout the trip and encouraged him to drink sips of water. Though his mouth was dry, the water burned going down and he could barely swallow the small sips his mother offered. Most often he simply held it in his mouth, allowing tiny amounts to trickle down his throat without swallowing. As the miles fell away behind them, the weakness overtook him; his bone-thin arms and legs became as heavy as lead weights.

Nurses met the family on arrival at the refugee camp and checked them for disease. As one of the sickest and most severely malnourished, Andrew was placed in a special tent—the tent of lost causes. His advanced cases of dysentery and malaria gave the medical personnel little hope that he would survive. He was placed in the tent of lost causes to die.

But Babcia and Zosia refused the nurses' verdict. They had not come through so much to lose young Andrew now. He would not die—they simply would not allow it. Many nights were spent in prayer beside his cot, many days were spent swabbing his fevered forehead and encouraging him to drink.

Sick with fever and exhaustion, young Andrew moved in and out of consciousness. On the cot beside him, a grown man moaned and shifted, his cot creaking loudly each time he moved. When the groaning stopped, a nurse came to check his pulse and then shook her head and draped the sheet over his head. Andrew knew the man had died. All night long he lay beside the corpse, ill and terrified. Certain that the body would rise and come to life, Andrew could not sleep.

A few hundred yards from the tent stood an old stone tower that aid workers had used to house the refugees who had lost their minds as a result of their intense suffering.

In this building they were placed, and at all hours of the day and night their cries, howls, and moans echoed through the young boy's body. "Help me!" the loudest among them cried through the night. "Help me, please!"

To ease his fears, Babcia spoke to Andrew. He heard her through the fevered haze in his mind. She spoke of God and all the miracles they had seen in Siberia. She told him that she would tell one last fortune today—Andrew's.

She crouched next to his bed, leaned close, and said, "I want you to know, Andrew, I saw that you will not die. Can you hear me? You will not die, but you will grow strong and big and do many good things in the world."

Babcia leaned against the cot of her weakened grandson and eventually dozed. When she awoke, Andrew was looking at her. "I saw grandfather," he said. "I stood up when I saw him, but he told me to get better. He said if I would lie back down and sleep, I would be all right."

Andrew became stronger every day. The nurses were amazed; they began to pay this miracle boy extra attention. After two weeks of steady improvement, Andrew was discharged from the tent of lost causes and moved back to his family's tent. And as Zosia and Babcia had predicted (nay, *willed!*), Andrew did not die—and here is yet another miracle of faith, determination and love, the final miracle from Siberia.

I DON'T REMEMBER much about that awful time of sickness. But I do remember that man dying beside me, and my fear keeping me awake all night. I remember staring at the mound beneath the sheet each time my eyes shifted, certain it was moving. I remember the incessant howls of the mentally ill patients chained in the nearby barn. I remember dreams in which my head swelled so big that it filled the tent and I was afraid it would explode. I remember seeing my grandmother sitting beside my cot when I awoke. I remember my little brother putting an orange in my hand—a precious and strange fruit given to him by the aid workers—and I remember the sweetness of its juice, the magic of it in my mouth. It was the only thing my brother had to give, it was something he cherished, and he gave it to me. I remember feeling in the tent that my grandfather was near. And I remember dreaming of wolves.

In Siberia, we believed in miracles. My mother and grandmother never lost hope. They firmly believed that we would survive and eventually return home. And so a miracle did happen: my father, who was a prisoner of war in Russia, was released and began searching for us.

And somehow, he found out where we were and commandeered a military truck with a driver. He plucked us out of that little village—I can still see the joy and shock and sadness on his own harrowed face—and settled us in a refugee camp near Iran, where families were being prepared to leave Russia. Within my family, our rescue was always considered a miracle, but it was a miracle that we never doubted would come.

My memories of Siberia have mostly faded away, supplanted by family stories told and retold for years until they became like legends. On a day-to-day basis, I don't remember much of Siberia. And yet, sometimes a smell or a sound will bring those memories flooding back, in vivid detail.

Moments ago, I stepped outside my home, into the cold of a western New York winter. Everything surrounding me was covered by snow and ice. The sharp tang of frigid air tickled my nose as I breathed it in. I closed my eyes and let the quiet envelop me until I could hear the wolves howling; I could feel my stomach clench with pangs of hunger; I could smell the sweet odor of dried manure burning in the hut behind me. Some days I relive it more than others. Writing this book has brought back many sensations and memories long buried and has made me even more grateful for the experiences of my life—yet another example of the teacher who learns, the giver who receives.

Of the five of us banished to Siberia—my grandparents, my mother, my brother, and I—I am the only one left. They have left this earth, one by one, and I have grieved at each new loss, but only for a time. Because what remains behind is love. The love we felt for each other; the powerful love that helped us to survive those difficult years. Love remains. It will never die.

I have had much love in my life and I am very fortunate. Without my grandfather's loving sacrifice, I would not be here today, would not be writing this. Of all the things that I have learned over the years, the most important is the knowledge that love is all that matters, and that with love, all things are possible.

As I approach the end of my life, I can see more clearly than ever what I learned in Siberia. I learned that we need love to survive, just as we need food and water. We need not only to *be* loved but also to love in return. And helping each other is one of the best ways that love is expressed.

My Siberian experiences inspired me to live the life that I have lived. They inoculated me against the disease of modern life—a disease we call *materialism*—and saved me from the "me first" philosophy that drives it. They helped me to understand that we are all connected, that we are all dependent on one another, that we must have courage, and hope, and kindness, and faith if we are to survive. And at the root of all those lessons is love. Love, pure and simple.

I want to leave you with a quotation from the ancient Greek dramatist Euripides, words that are still relevant many centuries after they were first written:

"Love is all we have, the only way that each can help the other."

EPILOGUE

AFTER LEAVING SIBERIA, my family and I spent a year in an Iranian refugee camp, then moved to Palestine where my father, Vincent Bienkowski, was stationed with British troops.

In 1947, we moved to England, where I learned to speak English at the age of thirteen. With the generous support of the British government, our family immigrated to the United States in 1948 and made a new life in upstate New York.

My father had been a lawyer in Poland, before serving in their armed forces. In America, the bar exam and a different legal system kept him from practicing law, but he found work as an office manager and thereby supported our family.

Sadly, the lingering effects of my mother's Siberian ordeal had left her weakened; she passed away in 1951 at the age of thirty-seven.

In the late 1950s, my grandmother reluctantly returned to Poland. Reluctantly, because she longed to be buried in the country of her birth, yet her beloved homeland was still not free of Communist rule. She died in Poland three years later.

In 1963, my father passed away peacefully at his home in Schenectady, New York, at the age of sixty-one.

My brother Jurek—"George" as he became known to his American friends—married, raised a family, and pursued a brilliant but tragically short career as a professor of mechanical and aerospace engineering at Princeton University. His talent in rocket design was put to use by the U.S. space program. In 1983 he traveled to Buffalo to compete in a grueling international marathon and stayed at my home. It was the last time we saw one another; Jurek was struck by a car and killed while training for a biathlon the following year.

I attended public school in upstate New York, and soon caught up to my fellow classmates. I graduated high school, joined the United States Air Force, and served for four years. At the end of my tour, I attended Union College in Schenectady and earned a Bachelor of Science degree. From there, I attended Western Reserve University in Cleveland and earned a Master of Science in Clinical Psychology. Thus began my long career of helping others.

I officially retired from clinical practice in 1996 but continue to teach classes and lecture on topics as diverse as overcoming fear, dream interpretation, and organic gardening. I also volunteer with my local hospice, providing compassionate end-of-life care for terminally ill patients and their families.

Me and my grandfather in Poland, about June 1939.

My grandfather, Vladislav, in Siberia. Taken February 1940, a month before his death.

My father in the Polish Army during WWII.

My mother, Zosia, 1950, a year before she died.

My parents and me in Poland,
circa 1938.

Me and my brother Jurek in
Poland, 1938.

My grandmother, Babcia, and her
daughter (my mother) Zosia,
Utica, NY, 1949.

Me, entering the United States Air
Force, 1953.

Questions and Topics for Discussion

1. ANDREW'S FAMILY OFTEN spoke of the "miracles" from Siberia. Which events from the book struck you as especially miraculous?

2. THE AUTHORS ENVISIONED this as a book that might be useful in a quest to help others. What take-away tools do you see yourself using in the future?

3. WHICH MEMBER OF Andrew's family did you find yourself relating most closely to, and why? Which chapter was your favorite, and why?

4. HOW CAN THE concept of "radical gratitude" help us to reframe our negative thoughts? Can you think of an example from your own life when something at first seemed like an unfortunate event but later benefited you in some way?

5. ANDREW'S FAMILY FOUND many creative ways to survive their years in Siberia. Which situation did you find most moving? Most clever? Most selfless?

6. DREAMS PLAY A very important role in this story. Do you listen to your dreams? Do you believe they can help you? Why or why not?

7. WHAT ROLE DO the wolves—fierce at times and peaceful at others—play in Andrew's life story? Would the story be the same without them?

8. PSYCHOTHERAPY MOSTLY INVOLVES "talking things out," and the author has said that his Siberia stories have lost much of their sting for him because he has told them so many times. Have you found this to be true of painful experiences in your own life?

9. FORGIVENESS IS AN important theme in this book. How might searching for the "radical gratitude" in a difficult situation help to lead one to forgiveness?

10. THIS BOOK HAS an unusual structure. Did the back-and-forth storytelling "work" for you as you read? Can you think of other examples from literature in which a story is offered as an illustrative "way in" to a moral message or instructive lesson?

ACKNOWLEDGMENTS

I OWE A great debt of gratitude to Bruce McCausland, who many years ago worked with me on the original version of this book. Many of the ideas in this book came from that period. But then the book sat in a drawer for years. My friends encouraged me to get going on it again, but my excuses were always that I can't write and I can't type. Then three things happened within a few days of each other. A friend, Barb Dadey, suggested that if I just wrote the book out in longhand, she would type it for me, free of charge. A few days later, Joy Herrick, another friend, told me that she knew someone who was a very good writer and might be interested in helping me with the book. That is how I met Mary Akers. I knew immediately that she was the right person to tackle this book. I learned that we are both Tauruses, and we hit it off from the first day. I admire Mary as a remarkable, loving human being who not only is a great writer but also a great mother and a talented teacher. I have no doubt that without Mary's writing skills, without her dedication and friendship, my story would not have been told.

So I want to honor and express gratitude to the four women who made this book happen. I think of them as the "four angels" of the book: Mary, Barb, Joy...and the fourth and most important angel is my wife Helen Schmidt, without whose love and support I would not have gotten very far. She is the star of my universe and I can't imagine my life without her in it.

I also want to thank the many friends who helped me in so many ways. They listened to me, encouraged me, made good suggestions, and they put up with me. Because I treasure their friendship and love and admire them, I am proud to put their names in my book. They are: Bill Schmidt, Andy McPherson, Ben Falcigno, Charlie Kung, Mary Lee Sulkowski, Gloria Knight, Joe Rautenstrauch, Gail Mellman, Joan Albarella, and last but not least, my two sons, Tim and Randy.

—Andrew Bienkowski

IN *any* HUMAN enterprise, there are so very many to thank when one considers the process from start to finish. I hope you will indulge me.

Chronologically, I should first thank Joy Herrick. She is the woman with the vision, the literary matchmaker who brought Andy's experience and my writing together. She is also a great cheerleader, encourager, and writer herself. Thank you, Joy; your parents named you well.

Andy, my coauthor, was a delight to work with. He never came to a session without bringing produce from his garden, a jar of his legendary homemade pesto, flowers, or a souvenir from his travels. He was encouraging and open to my changes but not afraid to tell me when I got it wrong— a valuable thing. It was *his* story, after all, and I often felt inadequate putting it in words, but he has said it felt as if I were "in his head, speaking for him," and I can't imagine finer words of praise.

Also, thank you to Andy's wife, Helen, who had me over on numerous occasions to celebrate our achievements, and always fed me well.

Isobel Dixon, our wonderful agent, believed in this project, even though it refused to fit neatly into one category for shelving. Is it memoir? Inspiration? Psychology? Self-help?

No matter; Isobel believed in our changeling child and in our ability to make something lovely out of what we had.

Thank you to Maggie Hamilton, who first took a chance on us, and to Matthew Lore, whose keen editorial eye has finally given us a voice in our own country. And to Ann Kirschner, copy editor extraordinaire, who showed me where I had missed the mark and helped me to find it.

I'd like to thank my fellow Queens alumni, among them, my good friends Tom Lombardo, Lu Livingston, and especially Cliff Garstang, my first, best, and last reader. Also Fred Leebron and Michael Kobre for starting and running such a wonderful, author-friendly MFA program.

I would be remiss if I didn't thank the Zoetrope Writers Studio, where I meet daily with my writer friends too numerous to name, but too helpful and supportive to leave out. Thank you all—in particular, Jessica Lipnack, who generously helped me when I panicked over writing my very first proposal.

I am grateful to the Second Monday Writing Group for listening and offering advice and support: Hallie Block, Elizabeth Glenny, Ann Goldsmith, Helen Weiser, Carolyn Epes, Anne Creaven, and Keith Inman.

To my mother, Sally Johnson, who helped me fine-tune the completed manuscript and provided support and encouragement along the way. My sisters, Sarah Samarchi and Helen Akers, for checking in and urging me to share my progress, and my brother, Tyler Akers, for moral support during a tough time, even though he doesn't like to do *touchy-feely*. And to my father, Frank Akers, for making reading an important part of my early years, and because he always wanted to see his name in a book.

Kevin Crosby at Full Circle Studios generously gave of his time and talents when I needed to quickly switch gears from print to video.

Laila Lalami for her loving support and guidance as the one who *got there first*.

Paula Bolte, Dawn Estrin, and Carolyn Green, who provided the sort of friendships that sustain a lonely writer, even long distance. And John Harkrader, who always believed in me, even when I was a gangly, scabby-kneed girl.

Because my conscience compels me, I need to offer quick thanks to the many people—both famous and unnamed—who indirectly contributed to the making of this book—people by which I have no other means to thank: the individuals whose personal struggles make up the case histories in this book, those who have lived through suffering in Siberia and elsewhere, those whose quotes served as a backdrop in the writing of this book and whose survival has made the world a better place; also, thank you to those who fight oppression and injustice wherever it is found. If I were to recount the entire genealogy of this book, my appreciations would be a never-ending list of teachers, friends, relatives, computer designers, papermakers, printers, Internet service providers, and more. But I cannot begin to touch all of those connections, so I will have to settle for a general sense of gratitude for the many lives that work and create and thereby sustain mine.

And last, but in no way least, I am infinitely grateful to my husband, Len, my constant source of strength (and favorite hiking companion), and my wonderful children, Charlotte, Cady, and Scott, who've put up with much along the way yet still get excited (and jump up and down with me) when I share good news.

—Mary Akers

ABOUT THE AUTHORS

ANDREW BIENKOWSKI, a veteran of the U.S. Air Force who served in the Korean War, worked as a psychologist for forty years, including thirty-two years for the State of New York, designing and implementing mental-health programs and working directly with patients. This is his first book. He lives near Buffalo, New York.

MARY AKERS's fiction, poetry, and nonfiction have appeared in many journals and anthologies. She is the author of a short-story collection, *Women Up on Blocks*, from Press 53. Although raised in the Blue Ridge Mountains of Virginia, which she will always call home, she currently lives in western New York.